Is that you, Maureen?

Is That You, Maureen?
My Life Making Children's Television & Beyond

First published July 2024 by Ten Acre Films Ltd.

ISBN 978-1-908630-86-5

Copyright © 2024 Jeremy Swan
Foreword copyright © 2024 Christopher Biggins
Afterword copyright © 2024 Anna Home

The rights of Jeremy Swan to be identified as the author of this work have been asserted in accordance with the Copyright, Designs and Patents Act 1988.

All rights reserved. No part of this publication may be reproduced, stored in or introduced into a retrieval system, or transmitted, in any form or by any means (electronic, mechanical, photocopying, recording or otherwise) without the prior written permission of the publisher. Any person who does any unauthorised act in relation to this publication may be liable to criminal prosecution and civil claim for damages.

A CIP catalogue record for this book is available from the British Library.

Project Editor: Stuart Manning
Indexing: Simon Guerrier
Printed in Great Britain by 4Edge Ltd.

This book is sold subject to the condition that it shall be not, by way of trade or otherwise, be lent, re-sold, hired out, or otherwise circulated without the publisher's prior consent in any form of binding or cover other than that in which it is published and without a similar condition including this condition being imposed on the subsequent purchaser.

Is that you, Maureen?

Written & Illustrated by
Jeremy Swan

TEN ACRE FILMS

Contents

THE TITLE	7
FOREWORD	9

1	CURTAIN UP!	13
2	THE MAKE-UP, THE COSTUMES, THE AUDIENCE, THE PROPS...	25
3	WHEN WORLDS COLLIDE	33
4	START SPREADING THE NEWS	39
5	YOU CAN ALWAYS SWITCH IT OFF	47
6	'JACKANORY, JACKANORY...'	53
7	PAR FOR THE COURSE	63
8	IN DUBLIN'S FAIR CITY...	67
9	'I HAVE RETURNED'	75
10	WHY DO THE WRONG PEOPLE TRAVEL?	79
11	CRIME AND PUNISHMENT	89
12	GOING SOUTH	97
13	SOME PEOPLE	105
14	DOWN UNDER	111
15	GOOSED	123
16	RAISED SETS	129
17	'MY OBJECT ALL SUBLIME'	137
18	SHE WHO MUST BE OBEYED	149
19	WORTH A LOT WHEN YOU'RE DEAD	155
20	TOM AND BLACKIE	161
21	CRUISING	167
22	FINISH UP	177

AFTERWORD	185
INDEX	188

This book is dedicated to the dedicated

The title

I was a producer/director of Children's TV programmes which were housed in a Stalinesque building in the BBC TV Centre called the East Tower. The East Tower was inconvenienced by the architecture, which placed the Ladies and the Gents' lavatories on alternative floors in the twelve-storey building.

A very eminent gentleman of the Board of Governors was caught short on a Ladies' loo floor. There was nothing for it but to nip into the nearest convenience. All the cubicle doors were open, except for a closed one at the end of the row. So, he nipped into the nearest, unzipped, and had the obligatory tinkle.

Whilst washing his hands he let rip with a blast of anal wind of such velocity that it echoed like a *thunderclap* around the porcelain and white-tiled walls.

A woman's voice asked behind the closed door at the end of the row...

"Is that you, Maureen?"

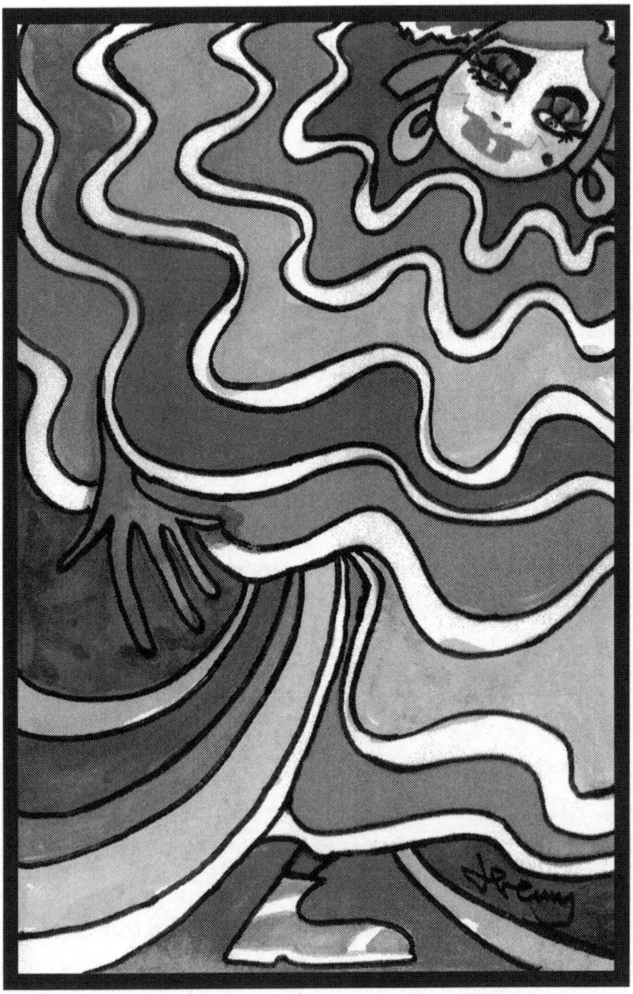

Foreword

by Christopher Biggins

Jeremy Swan is one of the funniest men I have ever had the pleasure of meeting and working with. It is with great pleasure that I write to say that his book is as funny — if not funnier — than him.

I recently went to a white-tie dinner at a mansion house in the city, full of Very Important People who were ever so excited to meet me because one of their favourite series was *Rentaghost* — which Jeremy, of course, produced and directed. I was thrilled because *Rentaghost* was one of the funniest shows I've ever had the pleasure of appearing in.

I played Adam Painting, the manager of the department store. One of my happiest memories involved Miss Popov, played by Sue Nicholls — star of *Coronation Street*. We were in a scene where something went wrong. In fact, something went very wrong.

I broke wind rather loudly. Sue and I were in the background of the scene and thought that Jeremy would let us go back and reshoot it. So we laughed, had a bit of a gossip, and eventually Sue caught the eye of our dresser and gestured to her that we would like two coffees.

At the end of this shambles, Jeremy announced, "Right! Next scene!"

"*No, no, no, no, no, no, no!*" Sue and I wailed.

"I passed wind!"
"We were corpsing!"
"I couldn't say my lines!"
"I wet my knickers!"
"It was all Biggins' fault!"

Jeremy's voice came over the Tannoy. "Let the audience and your agents see what amateurs you really are!"

The scene went out as recorded, with all our ridiculousness going on in the background. But we didn't mind because Jeremy Swan was a genius — and that genius has written this fabulous book.

Like Adam Painting and Miss Popov, you will never stop laughing.

Christopher Biggins
May 2024

Embellishment might constantly occur for the reader's delectation

ଔ

A Christmas card drawn by Micheál Mac Liammóir

Scene 1
Curtain up!

My life has been show business. And that's what I'll be writing about here, but not necessarily in that order — a series of happy digressions. Little scenes. Ups and downs, highs and lows. Mainly highs and ups.

I was born in Dublin, Ireland in 1941. Ireland is a land of legends: Finn McCool, Cú Chulainn, Deirdre of the Sorrows, Queen Maeve, the Children of Lir — and Micheál Mac Liammóir. He and Hilton Edwards founded the Gate Theatre in 1928. They were dear friends of my family, and affectionately known around Dublin as 'Sodom and Begorrah'.

In the 1960s, there was a supper party with my aunts — Sheila and Carmel Leahy — as the hostesses. My parents, me, and our friends 'The Pats' (famous artist Pat Scott and not-quite-so-famous actor Pat McLarnon), the Cassons, and Micheál and Hilton were the guests.

In the drawing room, Micheál pronounced, "I'm going to do a one-man show. Johnny G. is doing Shakespeare, Emlyn Williams is doing Dickens, so why not? And my darling Hilton will Direct."

Everyone exclaimed excitedly, "How wonderful! How marvellous!" All while thinking, *anything* is better than him repeating being a panto dame in the Gaiety.

"Who is this man going to be, Micheál?"

"It's going to be an Irish Writer."

"Terrific, Micheál! Will it be Congreve? Goldsmith? Brinsley Sheridan? Swift?"

This drew a moment's silence for an unfortunate recollection; the last time Mac Liammóir played Swift the critics described him as looking like Bette Davis in *What Ever Happened to Baby Jane?*).

Ireland's greatest actor drifted a beringed hand across his mascaraed eyes, dangerously tipping the toupee that rested like a black cliff above his rocky orange face. In his rolling brogue, cultivated from a suburban London accent, he pronounced, "It's going to be about Oscar Wilde."

This news was met with more drink pouring and a lot of gabble — "Great, Micheál, great!" — all while we thought, *Jesus*! It will be all green carnations, velvet pantaloons... will we ever forget the tights in *Othello*?"

Mac Liammóir's glittering eyes looked upwards at the Clery's lamp in the Leahy's drawing room. He pursed his lips, then further pronounced, "I'm going to call it *The Importance of Being Oscar*."

Of course he was. Hilton added that it would be performed before a captive audience.

It was. To the political prisoners in the Curragh Internment Camp.

The prisoners loved it, all politics aside, and *The Importance of Being Oscar* went on to become an international success — London, New York, everywhere — including Micheál's beloved Dublin.

Mac Liammóir had a devoted fan club entourage throughout Ireland. At the end of some performance at the Gaiety Theatre, he was informed that three sisters from Mallow in County Cork called O'Toole were waiting in the green room to say hello to their idol.

"I'd be *enchanted*," the idol told his dresser. He adored his provincial audience. "Please tell the darlings to wait!"

Waiting to meet a star was one of the most thrilling rituals in any fan's devotion. Being asked to wait was beyond thrilling; the longer the wait the better, as they awaited the Glorious Climax.

The Glorious Climax was Mac Liammóir taking off his stage make-up and putting on his street make-up — which was basically the same thing, though maybe a strata less. The eyes glittered beneath kohl-soaked lashes, a swift adjustment of the coal-black hairpiece — topped off with a squirt of mist of Guerlain's Mitsouko. The red silk kimono was tightened and a pungent French Gitane was lit — smoke mingling with the Mitsouko cloud. The painted god swept into the Green Room to meet the quivering faithful — who had now missed the last train to Mallow. No matter.

He kissed the hands of the sisters and melodiously told them of the glories of County Cork where he was brought up — insularly distant from his actual roots in north London. The sisters from Mallow were bewitched.

Emboldened to speak, one sister said she had a personal question for Mr Mac Liammóir. This was always a nervous moment for the star's dresser and attendants. Personal questions were always tricky.

"Please ask, Miss O'Toole," purred their idol.

"It's a question we'd all like to ask, if it's not too rude?"

He raised his boot-polished eyebrows to his pancaked forehead in a genial query and took another drag on the French fag.

Finally, Miss O'Toole asked, "Is Mrs Mac Liammóir in the theatre as well?"

* * *

Micheál Mac Liammóir was later made an honorary Doctor of Law by Dubin University. The phone rang at Harcourt Terrace where the boys lived.

"Could I speak to Doctor Mac Liammóir?"

Hilton answered. "This is Nurse Edwards — how can I help you?"

The Brendan Smith Academy of Acting had a Saturday morning children's class — which was an ideal way for parents to get their blasted kids out of the house for a couple of hours for the nominal cost of two shillings. My brother Nigel and I went. A lot of brats were recruited to be slum kids in *Liffey Lane* in the Gate, Nigel and I included. We weren't the most realistic casting because the slum kids didn't go to the Brendan Smith Academy on Saturdays, nor were Hilton and Micheál particularly aware of kids — let alone the slums. Nonetheless, *Liffey Lane* proved to be a great early taste of the theatre.

There were also plays put on by the Academy itself, performed at the Royal Academy of Music in Westland Row.

"I'm in a play," I told my parents.

"Great! What's it called?"

"It's called *The Magic Cuckoo Clock*. I'm to play Hans, the clock-maker's assistant. It's a terrific part. Can I borrow the cuckoo clock in the hall?"

A moment of deep suspicion. "What for?"

"To be the magic cuckoo clock!"

Daddy wasn't too enthusiastic. "That clock was a wedding present to your mother and me from your great-aunt Maud ten years ago. It's a family heirloom."

My mother prevailed on the persuasion of drama. She'd been an actress before she met Daddy, in the Torch Theatre in Dublin.

"OK."

Daddy said he would deliver the cuckoo clock for the first night to the Royal Academy of Music. He didn't want it lying around there in case it was pinched. I'd been rehearsing with a shoe box.

The first night arrived. In the theatre at Westland Row, Rossini's *William Tell Overture* scratched forth on speakers to get the audience into a suitably Tyrolean mood; the illiterate thought they were going to see *The Lone Ranger*. In the audience were Mummy, Daddy and my brother and sisters — Nigel, Naomi and Jacqui.

I was the eldest of the cygnets. Giselle, the youngest, hadn't been born yet. I was waiting in the wings, holding the family cuckoo clock — which felt like the size of Big Ben, while wearing lederhosen that seemed to be made of cardboard.

I was very, very nervous. I was to be the first one on, announcing, "The clock is finished, Master Johann."

Master Johann was already there, played by another little boy, made up to look like William Blake's interpretation of God the Father. The curtains squeaked open. The audience gasped — either at the set or the juvenile God the Father.

The gasp was my cue. On I went. My little sister, Naomi, sitting in the third row shouted out, "Hello, Jeremy!"

That got a huge laugh but I got a sudden shiver of fright and dropped the huge cuckoo clock. Its spectacular splintering brought the play to a dramatic halt. Mrs Brendan Smith rushed on, parallel to the closing curtains, armed with a tea chest, shovel and broom, to gather the remains of the Swan family heirloom.

"We will have to start again!" she bawled. "You'll have to use the shoe box."

"What about the cuckoo clock?" I squeaked.

"Pretend it's in the box!"

The Brendan Smith Academy of Acting was hot on improvisation.

The play started again. On I came with the shoe box. Another laugh unnerved me. I took a deep breath for my opening line and announced, "The *cock* is finished, Master Johann."

This prompted a bigger laugh and a smatter of clapping — sprinkled with vulgar guffaws. We staggered through the rest of the play, ending on enormous applause tinged with enormous relief. My father mended the cuckoo clock with tacks and glue and back it went on the wall. A mechanical flaw made the bird say "*Coo-cuck!*" ever after.

More plays followed. I was little Ricky Sherman in *The Seven Year Itch*, starring Milo O'Shea and Paula Byrne, directed by Godfrey Quigley at the Gaiety. Then came the part of the Dauphin's Page in George Bernard Shaw's *Saint Joan*, starring Siobhán McKenna — the First Lady of the Irish theatre.

Rehearsals were held at the Gaiety, directed by Hilton Edwards. There was a thrilling rumour that the Dauphin was to be played by Richard Harris — but he turned out to be in the slammer in Limerick for thrashing a pub. Hilton announced that, *pro tem*, the part of the Dauphin would be read by his partner, Micheál Mac Liammóir. Siobhán had just played Joan in London, where the Dauphin was a very young Kenneth Williams. The Dauphin was early twenties, according to Shaw. Mac Liammóir was 60 at the time.

As the rehearsals progressed, it became apparent that Richard Harris would *not* be playing the role.

After a Gaiety run came exciting news. The show would tour Europe, opening in Paris — and I was to go!

But what about school? I cracked that. I went to the Dean of Discipline in St Mary's College CSSp — *Congregatio Sancti Spiritus* — Rathmines, where I was enrolled.

"I know I've not been good in languages, religion instruction, geography, English literature and artistic appreciation."

"Yes," said Father Barry. "You're dreadful."

"The problem is solved!"

"How?" he asked coldly.

"I'm going on a European tour of *Saint Joan*, starring Siobhán McKenna, produced by the Dublin Gate Theatre — playing the Dauphin's Page to Micheál Mac Liammóir!"

"How wonderful!" exclaimed Father Barry. "Can we come to the dress rehearsal?" In those days, Catholic Priests could not go into public theatres.

Two weeks in the Gaiety and then off to Paris. I'd never been on a plane. Paris! *Magnifique!* We were to play the Théâtre de la Ville Sarah Bernhardt. I was also to be the assistant stage manager. At the rehearsals my job was to paint out the proclamation of Joan's declaration of heresy, to be read by Brother Martin. I got parchment paper and diligently — and calligraphically — wrote out the maid's denunciation in pen and ink, complete with wax seals. This was also done because Michael Murray, the actor, refused to bloody learn it.

To my horror, at the rehearsal Miss McKenna ripped the parchment to shreds, yelling, "Light your fire! Do you think I dread it as much as the life of a rat in a hole?"

Jumping Jesus — I'd have to do those proclamations for every night!

In Paris, the stage management, wardrobe department and I stayed on the top floor of a brothel in the Left Bank, off Saint-Michel. They were very nice girls who worked the evenings and were intrigued by young theatricals living above.

Meanwhile, the youthful Dauphin Micheál Mac Liammóir was down a tricky road. There was the initial perilous path of depicting the incoming King of France to France in France's capital city; this depiction began with a cheeky low-browed hat, eyelashes from here to Nottingham, a false nose and very high collar, slit to reveal pursed, rouged lips. The rest of the miracle was achieved by a rigid Rigby & Peller corset, performed with a lot of gambolling and creaky skipping with a cup-and-ball toy — better to emphasise the young Dauphin's juvenile traits.

It made the French audience sit up — as did Hilton Edward's direction of the piece. It was a great success. Hilton and Micheál summoned me to see them in the five-star George Cinq Hotel. I trotted across Paris from the brothel in the Rue de la Huchette.

"How are you?"

"Very well, thank you, Mr Mac Liammóir and Mr Edwards."

"Did you send a postcard to Una and Jack?"

They were my parents. "Yes."

"Did you send them our love?"

"Yes"

"How about school?"

Oh.

"Do you speak French yet?"

"I've only been here a week. I know 'oui', 'non' and 'merci'."

"Well, that's a start." Micheál declared. "Here's a Harrap French-English dictionary, a notebook and a pen. Down the Rue de Rivoli is the Louvre."

"What's that?"

"The reason there was a revolution in France. Go to the Louvre — in the door, up the stairs, and there you will see the Winged Victory." It was a Greek sculpture of a (since beheaded) angel. "Go no further! We want you to write an essay on the glories of the Winged Victory in French. In the notebook. With the pen and the dictionary and deliver it to me tomorrow."

Dear God in Heaven! I thought, this is getting a bit creepy.

"Have a croissant," said Micheál. "Mr Edwards can't eat them. He's getting too fat!"

At the Louvre, I wrote about the statue with the help of the museum's English guidebook and then diligently translated it into French from the dictionary — minus tense, with no grammar and useless adjectives — but the words were in fluent Harrap.

The next day I presented my scrawls to Micheál Mac Liammóir.

"This is indescribable," he intoned. "I will transcribe your writings in perfect French. You will transcribe what I write and tomorrow you will give me the transcription and then read it to me. I'll correct you. Did you send another card to Una and Jack?"

(In those days, there were no mobile phones to assist communication when abroad). Anyway, that's how I learned French.

The stage door keeper at the Théâtre Sarah Bernhardt had asked if I wanted any tickets for the first night. Unlikely. But then I had a thought.

"I'd like four."

Who for? The girls who worked below us in the Rue de la Huchette — two girls and a mother and a pimp. At the end of the triumphant first night, they were waiting for me at the stage door.

"Comme c'est *magnifique*! Incroyable, Joyeuse, *Mon Dieu!*"

"Would you like to meet Saint Joan?"

They spoke English due to their cosmopolitan clientele. I took them to Siobhán's dressing room. They genuflected and were awash with emotion. She almost blessed them while sipping a gin and tonic.

"Nice to meet you all," she said in her Mayo brogue. "Are you going home now?"

"No," the girls replied. "We're going back to work."

"Work?"

"*Mais oui*, we have customers waiting!"

From Paris, we went to Holland to Germany to Italy.

In The Hague, Queen Juliana attended the Dutch first night. Protocol demanded that we bowed left first to the royal box and then out front to the audience. Reginald Jarman, another actor in our company, mistakenly bowed to the right and caused a mild diplomatic frisson.

We travelled around Holland by coach from The Hague to Amsterdam to Utrecht. Micheál looked out of the window and airily declared that he had just seen a little boy with his finger in a dike.

We flew from Holland to Italy, stopping to change planes in Frankfurt. Looking out of the window, we saw there was a huge crowd at the airport.

"Ah, bless Deutschland!" said Mac Liammóir. Not many did — it was 15 years after the war ended. "They remember my Judge Brack with Peggy Ashcroft in *Hedda Gabler* in Berlin."

"They do not!" declared the First Lady of the Irish Theatre. "They remember my Pegeen Mike in *The Playboy of the Western World*!"

Blessed Deutschland remembered neither.

Elvis Presley drove past the plane in an open jeep, waving to the masses.

"Look! Look!" we cried. "It's Elvis!"

"Elvis who?" asked Mac Liammóir, coolly.

Elvis Presley was doing his military service with the US troops in Germany. We landed in Bologna and got on a bus to drive us through the night to Florence. The tour was being run on somewhat economic lines.

The Renaissance splendour of Florence staggered me. I bought my mother a vivid raffia bag at the market. We played at the Teatro della Pergola.

Among the wardrobe staff was Kay Casson, the daughter-in-law of Dame Sybil Thorndike, the first Saint Joan in Shaw's play. Her husband — not Dame Sybil's — Christopher Casson was playing the Inquisitor. His father, Sir Lewis Casson, had played the part originally. Kay and her colleague Betty Long complained of the inadequate laundry facilities at the medieval theatre. "It was impossible to get things dry," moaned Kay Casson.

"I *know*," whinged Reg Jarman. He was a major whinger. "My tights were still wet!"

"That's funny," snapped Mrs Casson. "We didn't wash yours!"

Micheál Mac Liammóir took Betty Long to one side. "I'd be very careful, darling Betty, walking around the streets of Firenze with your voluptuous figure and swarthy appearance. It could attract unwelcome attention."

"Speak for yourself, dear," said Miss Long, tartly.

Micheál took me on a walking tour of Florence, extolling about the Medicis, Michelangelos and the rest of the Florentine cast. We stopped in the middle of the Piazza della Signoria and he pointed dramatically at the ground. "*This*," he boomed, "is where Savonarola was burned."

This was another education trap.

"Who?" I asked.

The trap snapped shut.

"I want a 200-word essay in English and Italian about Savonarola and his principles delivered to my dressing room tomorrow in the Teatro Della Pergola!"

The exercise gave me a smattering of Italian — *grazie, dottore!*

We were then on to Switzerland to play at the Schauspielhaus Theatre in Zürich. Throughout our tour, we were feted by the Irish Embassies in each country. The legendary diplomat Josephine McNeill was our hostess at one do. I resisted buying a cuckoo clock for my father in Switzerland. Instead, I settled for a carved wooden statue of a cow with a bell around its neck.

The *Saint Joan* tour gave me a deceptively impressive CV, having worked at so many major European theatres.

St Mary's College welcomed me back. I was given big parts in the school plays after the tour. I had glamour and notoriety — mainly in drag roles. I was my brother's mother in *The Winslow Boy*; Nigel was the Winslow Boy. Father Barry was the director. He forbade the boys playing his female characters from having tits — fearing that such adornments would lead to transvestism. I inserted knockers while playing Lucy in *The Rivals* and nearly got expelled.

St Mary's College school hall wasn't quite the Théâtre Sarah Bernhardt. But we did good plays, including *The Only Way* — a dramatisation of *A Tale of Two Cities* with a spectacular guillotine.

After school, I inevitably went into the theatre; at first as an ASM — assistant stage manager — and the occasional acting role, including *Auntie Mame*. Marie Conmee, a large actress, played the lead; I was her nephew. Marie was so butch that everyone thought I was playing Mame.

Marie Conmee and her companion, Mrs Mary Brady were christened Mr and Mrs Al Capone by fellow actor Patrick McLarnon.

As an actor at the Gate, I played a servant, a soldier, some bloody child and a tree. In *Macbeth*, as a servant, I had to walk across the stage with a tray of fruit, making the Macbeths — Godfrey Quigley and Iris Lawler — dramatically pause from sinisterly plotting their murder. In this tense moment, I unfortunately let my eyes swivel to the audience. Or maybe it was my walk? My legs were overlong, encased in baggy tights. Or maybe it was the wig? But anyway, I got a laugh and I got fired!

The penny was beginning to drop. I was a lousy actor.

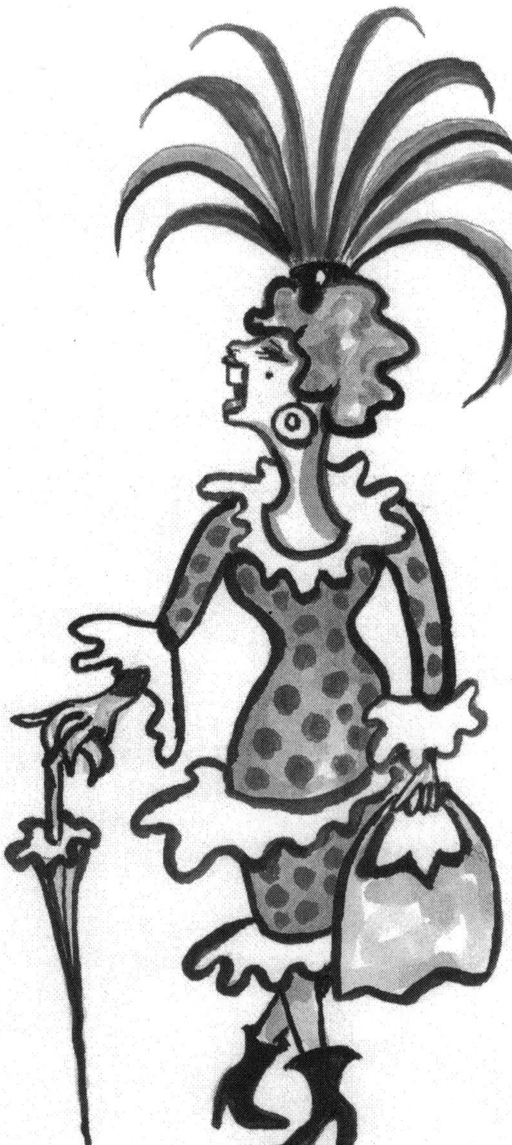

Scene 2

The make-up, the costumes, the audience the props....

I decided it was best to walk off the stage and into the wings. From now on, I did stage management and props and prompting — that sort of thing — and the odd walk-on part. I'd wheedled my way back into the Gate as an ASM, and assistant to Lona Moran, the set designer.

One day, we waited for some play's rehearsal to finish, armed with buckets of paints and brushes to get on with an unfinished set. They were blocking a scene when Ann Rowan — a character actress and delightful drinker who starred in the RTÉ soap opera *The Riordans* — was to make her entrance. Miss Rowan, I suspected, had had a Cork gin or five at the lunch break. She was to come through the open door with a shopping bag and an umbrella.

"On you come, dear." directed the director, Barry Cassin.

On she came.

"Hold it!" commanded Mr Cassin.

"*Whaaaat*'s the matter, *lovvve*?" She had a sort of purry voice.

"When you come through the door you have to close it afterwards."

"Ah darling, pet, but how can I close it? I've got the shopping bag in one hand and an umbrella in the other."

"Hold the umbrella and the bag in one hand and close the door with the other."

"Alright, pet. I'll try it again," she purred.

"You don't have to — just remember to close the bloody door when you come on."

"Ah Cassie, darling! It's all very well for you but I'll be the one in front of the audience. I'll have to try it again. To get it spot on."

So off she went. Barry Cassin was beginning to seethe. She called him 'Cassie Barrin', much to his irritation.

"On you come, Ann," Cassie Barron seethed. There was much fumbling behind the door. Finally, it opened and she came through with the props in one hand. She turned to close the door and dropped the props.

"Ah, Jesus! This is tricky business, Cassie."

She picked up the props.

"I'll have to try it again."

"Oh, for fuck's sake!" directed Mr Cassin. "Try it again."

She tried again, this time managing to shut the door.

"You won't believe it, darling — I've forgotten what I do next with the bag and the umbrella!"

"You put the bag on the table and hook the umbrella to the back of the chair!"

"But angel, *sweetheart*... How can I do that when I'm holding them both in one hand?"

"You transfer the umbrella to the hand with which you have closed the fucking door!"

Meanwhile, our paint was hardening. Lona and I were now getting a bit pissed off with all this artistic creativity.

Mrs Rowan sighed. "I'd better try the entrance again. This is getting very technical, love."

THE MAKE-UP, THE COSTUMES, THE AUDIENCE, THE PROPS...

Other actors were waiting to continue playing the scene. On went the business with the closing door, shopping bag, umbrella, chair and table.

On the first night, Ann Rowan made her entrance to a ripple of applause — she was very popular. She closed the door, hooked the umbrella on the back of the chair. Things were on course with the dialogue.

"Good to see you, Agnes. Where have you been?"

Miss Rowan was playing Agnes.

"Shopping."

"What did you buy?"

"It's in the ba—!"

✱ ✱ ✱

I was ASM on *Hedda Gabler* at the Gate for Longford Productions. Lord Longford shared half the year with Hilton and Micheál as part of some Gate Theatre bail-out arrangement.

Hedda Gabler is not one of Norway's theatrical side-splitters.

To accentuate the domestic oppression of the drama, the director and the designer set the piece in a gloomy basement apartment — a staircase on stage left indicated the Tesman family's house above. Staircases on stage were tricky because they meant a ladder was needed in the wings for the actors to scale and descend onto stage. This was particularly difficult for Hedda, played by Miss Iris Lawler in a flouncy dress with a bustle.

The set was illuminated by a pale barred window looking out to a wall, topped by a misty pine tree garden.

The end of the play depicted Hedda menacingly crossing the stage with her father's shotgun, leaving the assembled company and exiting through a door on stage-right on the OP (opposite prompt) side, with the intention of blowing her brains out.

I told you it was a side-splitter.

Hedda left the stage. The OP side of every theatre usually had bottles lined up against the wall — beer bottles, disgusting milk bottles left over from the beverages of the stage crew, plus other glassy detritus. Miss Lawler had exited to fire the blank that would scare the shit out of the audience and end the play. She had insisted on firing herself, distrusting the stage management, in case they fucked up Hedda's final moment.

Click.

"Shit!" *click-click*, "Shit, shit! Fuck!" I heard from the prompt corner.

Not Ibsen. The gun had jammed.

The audience couldn't hear the clicking and expletives. Miss Lawler, in the isolation of the OP side, hurled the gun in fury at the bottles. There was an explosion of glass shattering. The last line of the play came.

"Good God, it's Hedda! Ordinary people don't do that."

The director, Christopher Casson added, "And she's jumped out of the window!"

The curtains closed on the basement set.

* * *

Enough of the stage. On to motion pictures and happy days spent at Ardmore Studios in Bray, County Wicklow. I was mostly an extra — you didn't have to act as an extra, just be an extra. At a tender age, I had to cross a bridge in *Captain Lightfoot*, starring Rock Hudson, Barbara Rush and Jeff Morrow. My auntie Kay was madly in love with Rock Hudson — a hopeless infatuation.

I did a lot of background work in *Shake Hands with the Devil*, which starred James Cagney, Don Murray, Dana Wynter, Michael Redgrave and Glynis Johns. We called Glynis 'Guinness Johns' because of her liking of the national brew. She was entitled to drink — her husband Anthony Forwood had run off to live with Dirk Bogarde.

I became a 3rd assistant director at Ardmore.

Irish show business in the 1950s was very incestuous. It was inevitable that when Irish Television started — first called Montrose Studios and renamed Raidió Teilifís Éireann — that most of the new technicians would be graduates of the Dublin Theatres and Ardmore Studios. Hilton Edwards became the Head of Drama. There was a cruel rhyme of the time:

> *There was an old man of Montrose*
> *with small eyes and a very big nose.*
> *He did plays by the score*
> *By Mac Liammóir —*
> *That silly old man of Montrose!*

THE MAKE-UP, THE COSTUMES, THE AUDIENCE, THE PROPS...

Actually, the silly old man didn't. Brilliant Hilton recruited talent from the theatre, such as the legendary Shelah Richards of Abbey fame — I was her lodger at Greenfield Manor, across the road from RTÉ. From the BBC, Hilton recruited director Chloe Gibson — immortal for the expression 'camp as Chloe' and for discovering Dirk Bogarde. Chloe took to Ireland fervently and became an ardent Roman Catholic. Hilton Edwards said, "Chloe is not so much a convert but more a pervert to Catholicism!"

The Assistant Head of Drama was Brian Tobin, Micheál Mac Liammóir's friend. Mac Liammóir called him 'Horus of the Birds' — an Egyptian mythical simile based on the fact that Brian had worked for Aer Lingus. A few other refugees from Aer Lingus, all ex-air hostesses, flew to RTÉ. Edith Cusack became Head of Women's Programming; Brendan Neilan became RTÉ's casting director. Maeve Conroy was Head of Children's Programmes — I don't know where she came from but had a good Irish name. That went slightly askew when she became Mrs Pujorski after marrying a Pole.

The Controller of Programmes was Michael Barry, an Englishman but with a suitably authentic Cork name. RTÉ was very nationalistic back then; such Celtic nominations later went out of the window when he was replaced by Gunnar Rugheimer, an enthusiastic Swede. Michael Barry, enthusing in the local vernacular, greeted Hilton, his Head of Drama: "Top of the morning to you, Hilton! And, tell me, how is Me Hole?"

I was recruited as a lighting assistant, a frightful job which necessitated clamping huge lamps to the scaffolding grid high above the studio sets. Our initial makeshift soundstages were at the Merrion Hotel in Ballsbridge and then a studio in Dublin's Abbey Street, which was owned by Eamonn Andrews, the Chairman of RTÉ. These *pro tem* locations were while the new facilities were being built in Donnybrook.

At the new studios, I was transferred to work in the sound department, where I had to play records. That transfer ended abruptly when I put the six o'clock Angelus bell on at the wrong speed. It sounded like the fire brigade. I was exiled back to clamping lights.

Yawn. This is getting a bit chronological — riveting though the dawn of RTÉ is...

***

Jump forward, Jeremy! I left RTÉ in 1966, provoked by their refusal to interview me for a director's job. I'd become a floor manager. This refusal was further incensed by an encounter with a frightful geek I'd been at St Mary's College with, in the RTÉ reception area.

"Eugene, how fabulous to see you! What's been happening to you?"

"I went away to be a priest but then discovered that I didn't have the vocation."

"Ah, tough shit! Why are you here?"

"I'm being interviewed for a director."

Jumping Jesus — here was someone even God rejected! I saw red and promptly got a floor manager job with Granada TV. (My granny heard the news and gave me a Spanish dictionary — no, not that Granada, Nana!)

Manchester in the 1960s was known as the City of 500 Night Clubs.

But I didn't go to nightclubs.

I lived in a penthouse across from the studios, thanks to running into Don Bennetts, an ex-RTÉ director and Australian friend, in the foyer of Granada's when I was being interviewed. He had enormous style and a spare room in the penthouse where he lived with his girlfriend, Vanya Kewley. She wasn't too pleased to see a Swan in her love nest. She was a newscaster for Granada. He directed documentaries for the station.

Don had enthusiastically prologued my visit with lovable descriptions of Jeremy's flamboyance, his dancing, his singing, his colourful clothes, his artistry...

It took one second for Vanya's cunning journalist brain to join the dots: "Faggot! Boyfriend? Raving queen!"

Happily, those barriers were swiftly dismembered and the three of us settled into a harmonious and hilarious existence. Well, it wasn't quite so harmonious when they started to have lively spats over trivial and intense matters. The hilarity abated tensely.

There was a party to celebrate the sixth birthday of *Coronation Street*, the jewel of Granada's crown. I'd become the floor manager of England's most popular soap. Don was away documenting Morocco with presenter Chris Kelly and left Vanya smouldering in the penthouse while I went off to the party...

BRACE
YOURSELF FOR
GREATNESS
THE BOOK
THE WORLD
COULD NOT
LAY DOWN
IS NOW A
MOTION
PICTURE.
PARAMOUNT PICTURES PRESENTS
RICHARD BURTON
CLAIRE BLOOM
OSKAR WERNER
THE SPY WHO
CAME IN FROM
THE COLD
A MARTIN RITT
PRODUCTION
Co-starring
SAM WANAMAKER
GEORGE VOSKOVEC · RUPERT DAVIES · CYRIL CUSACK and PETER VAN EYCK ·
Produced and Directed by MARTIN RITT
Screenplay by
PAUL DEHN and GUY TROSPFR ·
Based upon the novel "THE SPY WHO CAME IN FROM THE COLD" by JOHN LE CARRÉ
Music Composed and Conducted by SOL KAPLAN
A SALEM
PRODUCTION
A PARAMOUNT PICTURE

Scene 3

When worlds collide

I'll digress here, to distract from the wobbly harmony of Manchester and to recall a life-enhancing experience of two years earlier. *The Spy Who Came in from the Cold* was being filmed in Dublin — adapted from John Le Carre's book, starring Richard Burton. Word came out on the Rialto that assistant directors were required for night shooting. I *had* to work on it, despite floor managing RTÉ's soap *The Riordans* — surely I could manage both? After all, night shooting meant that the Riordan family would be asleep.

I got the job — 5th assistant director for the night shoots on *The Spy*. What does a 5th assistant director do? I was the last one in line to shout out, "Quiet!"

The art department had taken over a large square in Smithfield, in the slums of Dublin, for the reconstruction of Berlin's 'Checkpoint Charlie'. Lampposts were specially imported from Germany. This enormous set was for the crucial opening scene of the film. Alec Leamas, the spy played

IS THAT YOU, MAUREEN?

by Richard Burton, was to wait in the Checkpoint Charlie kiosk for the arrival of an agent on a bicycle in the bleak Berlin night. An immense camera track was built, stretching across the Square; it had taken days. Eventually, it was ready to be surveyed by the director, 'Hollywood legend' Martin Ritt.

"Fetch the director," yelled Colin Brewer, the 1st assistant director — and my boss. He was so tough he made Stalin look like Su Pollard.

This command was bawled down the line until it stopped at me. I went to the director's Winnebago — a vehicle the size of Victoria Station — parked in a site adjacent to the Square. After my timid knock, the creative brains of the movie emerged. There was Angela Martelli, the greatest Continuity girl in the world; a producer who was Paul Newman's brother, dressed as a Nazi Stormtrooper (don't ask); the director's assistant — a beautiful Swedish girl who spoke no English; a young American with a tray containing suitable libations for the strenuous two-minute walk to the set; and finally Mr Ritt, waddled out swathed in blankets, smoking a cigar with a paddy cap on his head. I lead this colourful assembly to the set. Mr Ritt looked at the huge scaffolding bridge track, going diagonally right to left across the square. His eyes had narrowed behind his shaded specs if we could have seen them.

"I want it the other way round. Not right to left! *Left to right!*"

And with that, they all marched back to the Winnebago.

The pronouncement caused a bit of merry hell.

Three more days of hammering, clanking, shifting and curses followed. These long nights followed my days working on *The Riordans* — helped enormously by Dexedrine, which made you awake when you were asleep.

Three days later, the track now went from left to right. And the brilliant Art Department had transformed the Square into our German No Man's Land. The residents of the Square — who could be described, in majority, as feral — were given wads of cash to block out their tenement windows and make themselves scarce. Unfortunately, the wads were distributed somewhat early in the evening, so they all got plastered on Red Biddy, a local liqueur. They then attempted to hinder the work of the great lighting man, Oswald Morris, by hanging mirrored wardrobe doors, screaming babies and grannies out of the windows, while demanding more dosh — all while singing lusty choruses of *In Dublin's Fair City* and *The Minstrel Boy*.

"Blimey," a seasoned spark growled. "It wasn't like this on *The Guns of Navarone!*"

Order was brutally and aquatically restored by the Dublin Fire Brigade, on hand to supply an artistic glistening to the buildings. Cranes were then used to hoist the camera dolly up onto the track. During all this, I'd been standing around doing nothing. I didn't mind. I was being paid an unbelievable £25 per night.

At last, we were ready! The opening shot was lined up, with Richard Burton's stand-in in the Checkpoint Charlie kiosk. There was no sign of the star. He was in Dublin's Gresham Hotel Penthouse Suite with his new bride, Elizabeth Taylor. They had just completed *Cleopatra* in Rome where they had fallen in love. The current Mrs Burton had played the Serpent of the Nile. She had been pursued by her ex-husband, Eddie Fisher, to Rome but to no avail. His newish, Jewish wife was still in love with him; Fisher had been married to Debbie Reynolds who said when he ran off, "I made one big mistake in Hollywood. I forgot to lock my husband in the garage the day I asked Elizabeth Taylor to lunch."

Back to the kiosk, where the camera was lining up. Richard Burton's double was standing in for Richard Burton's stand-in and also doubling for Richard Burton in the kiosk.

The Dublin night air was brittle with tension. A mansion in the square, belonging to the Jameson whiskey family, had been annexed to become Richard Burton's dressing room. The Jamesons had been sent on holiday to Florida.

The Irish Army had been recruited as Stasi soldiers — part of a government deal for the film being shot in Ireland and because the IRA was having a bit of a lull. Richard Burton eventually made it to the kiosk, glittering with hangover, as demanded by the script — and methodically achieved by the star. What a pro!

A low camera had to squeeze in the kiosk to capture Burton's close-up — plus a cameraman and Mr Burton's dresser, poised for any emergency that might befall face or frock. The main camera for the master shot was high above on the dolly, sitting on the scaffolding track.

A Hollywood stuntman was to cycle through the frontier point and then get shot dead. Invisible wires were tied around him, ready to be tautened on cue, so that his body would twist and turn on bullet impact. It was a lot of fuss.

"There's no easy way to do this," my sparks friend said, sagely.

"Yes, there is," his mate replied. "Use real fucking bullets!"

All this action needed to be seen over Richard Burton's shoulder on camera. He wanted to sit down while making his exhausting observation, so a high stool was asked for and magically produced. The star had to get out of the kiosk for the stool to be got in. This was manoeuvred in and around the bodies of the cameraman, the make-up man and Mr Burton's dresser, lying down on the floor while Burton sat on the stool. His breath needed to be seen, so lights had to go into the kiosk, held up by a huge electrician who lay on top of the already prone trio. There were screams and snapping of limbs heard but nobody minded. It was a mute shot.

The clapperboard was poised. At last, we were about to go for a take.

There was a disturbance in the distant crowd, who were jostling to see the filming behind barriers and a phalanx of policemen. A big green Rolls Royce could be seen coming through the barricades. The first assistant director went into major Tourette mode. Mr Ritt bit through his cigar.

Richard Burton staggered out of the kiosk, trampling those underfoot and looked joyfully at the approaching limo. "It's Lilibeth! It's my little girl!" he cried.

Everything ground to a halt. Frissons of excitement ran through the crew — though not through the first assistant director nor Mr Ritt.

"She's here. She's actually here!" we thought. We're going to see the star of *Little Women, Father of the Bride, Giant, Cat on a Hot Tin Roof... Lassie Come Home!* The ex-Mrs Hilton, the ex-Mrs Wilding, the widow Todd, the ex-Mrs Fisher and the current Mrs Burton — all rolled into one.

The Rolls purred to a halt near the kiosk. Gaston, the chauffeur opened the door. He was a somewhat disgraced figure, having knocked down a Dublin mother with the Rolls; his employer had slightly assuaged the incident by gifting the unfortunate woman and her family 24 bicycles. Out of the limo stepped Elizabeth Taylor, looking exactly like Cleopatra — except wearing a mink anorak and lime-green trews. On her head was a Nefertiti-type hat, only adding to her regal air.

The couple embraced. She snuggled up to him, her famous violet eyes swivelling about. Burton's catty dresser whispered to me that she was only there in case Burton's co-star Claire Bloom was hanging around. Miss Bloom had played Ophelia to Burton's Hamlet at the Old Vic decades ago and, as is every Hamlet's prerogative — with the exception of Sir Ian

McKellen, Sir John Gielgud and Micheál Mac Liammóir — Burton had embarked on a fling with his Ophelia.

There were no flies on the new Mrs Burton. As ballast, she'd brought a load of kids — some her own, some from other husbands, some adopted from Vietnam. Suddenly, came a terrifying command! Elizabeth Taylor wants fish and chips! In the middle of the night! In the slums of Dublin!

"Do it!" snarled Burton.

With more wads of cash, a fish and chip shop was found nearby. The owners were woken up. the oil pans were heated up and the cod and chips were fried. I escorted Miss Taylor to the chippy. She linked my arm.

"I hope I'm no trouble" she whispered.

"Never!" I declared — a statement which would be vehemently denied by the producers of *Cleopatra*, several of whom were dead from premature heart attacks thanks to Madam No Trouble.

"Keep up, kids!" she yelled behind her, transforming from Cleopatra into Martha from *Who's Afraid of Virginia Woolf?*

A Phoenix in the rain

Scene 4

Start spreading the news

What did I do with all the money? I went to New York and stayed in the Algonquin Hotel. There I called up Geraldine Fitzgerald, the niece of Shelah Richards — my Dublin landlady and a big Hollywood star. Geraldine lived on Park Avenue with her husband Boy Scheftel, who owned Macy's and a waxworks museum. Geraldine received me very enthusiastically, wanting to hear news of her aunt and Dublin. She had people in the apartment and introduced me as her aunt's lodger.

In the room were Bette Davis, Rod Steiger, the director Sydney Lumet, famed Broadway caricaturist Al Hirschfeld and his daughter Nina. Bette Davis was puffing away on a cigarette. "Hi," she puffed.

I told Rod Steiger I'd just been working with his wife, Claire Bloom, and Richard Burton. Rod's eyes took on the same swivel as Elizabeth Taylor's. Sydney Lumet had just directed *The Pawnbroker*, starring Geraldine and Rod Steiger. Al Hirschfeld told me his daughter's name Nina, was in all his cartoons. It is — look out for it in the line of a subject's hair or the folds of their costume.

From New York, I went to San Antonio, Texas, to see Maureen Halligan — my old boss in lots of Dublin productions — now working in the Santa Rosa Medical Center in San Antonio. Maureen was always drawn to religion. Her boss was Sister Mary Vincent, a dynamic nun who filled me in with lurid descriptions of JFK's assassination. She had lots of creepy theories. As a result of these, she was swiftly moved to a convent in the west of Ireland where her treasonous whispers would only fall on Connemara stone walls.

Maureen had checked me into the St Anthony Hotel. On the terrace, under a yellow Texan sky, I sat having a solitary drink — gin and tonic; Sauvignon Blanc had not yet been invented. A waiter came over to me.

"The lady would like to offer you a drink."

The lady was a few tables away — dark glasses and a big hat.

"How nice, thank you."

With the drink in hand, I went over to the lady and thanked her. She asked who I was, and how did I come to be in San Antonio.

"Irish. Made a lot of money on a film."

She said, "I made money in films. That's why I live here."

She was Pola Negri, the great silent movie star. A lovely, faded lady. I took her to dinner at the Blue Bonnet across the street. She'd never been there — a silent screen recluse exiled by the arrival of talking films.

But enough of digressions, Jeremy. Get back to the plot!

***

The penthouse in Manchester. A party for the sixth birthday of *Coronation Street*. Great gas with actors Pat Phoenix, Bill Roach, Philip Lowrie, Violet Carson, Margot Bryant, Doris Speed — and Tony Warren who created the show, presided by Sydney Bernstein who owned Granada. I was very far down the pecking order.

The party was in a room whose windows opened onto a car park. There was a screech of brakes and the hooting of a car horn...

***

Another digression — oh for God's sake, Jeremy! — But slightly *á propos...* I've just had a call from Sue Nicholls — still on *Coronation Street* in 2023 playing Audrey. We go back years. Sue first worked for me in a BBC TV musical *When Santa Rode the Prairie* ('When the West was wild and hairy'). It was written by Willie Rushton, with songs by Roy Civil. Sue and Pamela Charles and Victor Spinetti starred. Of course, Sue and I talked fondly about *Rentaghost* — a show I produced for BBC Children's TV.

I inherited that series from Paul Ciani, a brilliant BBC producer who left the BBC to work in Singapore. It was a show about ghosts. Monica Sims, the glorious Head of BBC Children's Programmes, commanded me to direct an episode of *Rentaghost* while Paul was having his interview for the job in Singapore.

OK. I looked at a rehearsal in the North Acton BBC rehearsal rooms and then set off for the BBC studios in Birmingham where the series was shot. I sat down in the control room, very nervous. Everyone was very suspicious of me — worse still, the cast. After we recorded the first scene, I wanted to record it again. "Why?" rightly demanded the floor manager, David Crichton.

"Well, don't tell them, but if we do it again, they might be a bit quicker!"

David liked that. He bellowed, "You were all too bloody slow, so we'll do it again — quicker!"

The suspicious cast seemed to like that too.

Paul Ciani was meant to turn up to take over from me in the afternoon. He did turn up but didn't take over. He was plastered with the exuberance that he'd got the job in Singapore. The upshot of Paul's great career sweep was that the blessed Monica Sims put me in charge of *Rentaghost*.

"You'll direct the next series," she commanded.

"Do you mind if I make a few changes?"

"Do what you like. We'll be only running it for one more season."

I made the changes. It vigorously ran for another eight series.

My PA, Susie Needle, upped my credit to producer.

"But I'm not a producer." I squeaked, "I'm only a director!"

"You're a producer now, sweetheart."

I quickly fell in love with *Rentaghost*. An old boom operator came up to me at some do a while back. "Ah, *Rentaghost*," he said. "We all used to love working on that. All those OTT actors bawling their lines out front!"

I'd have preferred a more cutting-edge comment on my directorial skills

— but he did say, "We all loved working on that."

Everyone did. It was the greatest gas. A dear, loyal cast and a brilliant writer, Bob Block. Bob was an unassuming, bespectacled man — totally above suspicion for the madness, mischief and mayhem that emerged from his pencil. He hand-wrote the scripts and his wife, Madeleine, typed them up in camera-script format for our convenience. My loyal assistant David Crichton — the son of legendary Ealing comedy director Charles Crichton — directed the film inserts and ran the studio floor.

In the North Acton rehearsal rooms, trying to coordinate twelve adults jumping in the air, pinching their noses so they could disappear in a jump cut, took a lot of jumping before we achieved synchronisation. A weeping Christopher Biggins hysterically laughed, "I can't believe we're getting paid for this!"

"Neither can I," I barked. "Jump again!"

The cast of *Julius Caesar*, rehearsing on the floor below, weren't best pleased with the thunderous thumps on the ceiling.

The original *Rentaghost* trio of spooks was Michael Staniforth as Mr Claypole, Michael Darbyshire as Mr Davenport, and Anthony Jackson as Mr Mumford. Betty Alberge and John Dawson played Mumford's perplexed living parents. Edward Brayshaw and Ann Emery were the ghosts' manager, Mr Meaker, and his wife Ethel. I brought Ann in after the first series, as I thought we needed more women. The regulars in our cast swelled with the arrival of the Meakers' beleaguered neighbours Mr and Mrs Perkins, played by Jeffrey Segal and Hal Dyer, and Molly Weir as Hazel the McWitch.

When Tony Jackson decided to leave and Michael Darbyshire died unexpectedly and unfortunately, we added Tamara Novak, a hayfever-afflicted nanny ghost played by the wonderful Lynda Marchal. Lynda's character worked well and the audience loved her — so I wasn't overjoyed when she said she wanted to leave after one series.

"Leave!? To do what?"

"Write."

"Write what?"

Lynda Marchal, the very talented actress, left to become Lynda La Plante, the super-talented writer.

The nanny character was magnificently recast with Sue Nicholls as Miss Popov. She had a 'little bit' in *Coronation Street*, so we had to work around that. The little bit is still going strong forty years later.

We rehearsed the shows from Monday to Thursday in North Acton. On Friday evening, we'd record the episode in studio, having camera rehearsed all day. The evening recording was planned to go without a hitch. All horrors had been ironed out during the camera rehearsal.

The first scene had to include the opening titles and signature tune; this was preceded by a countdown on the VTR clock. On one notorious occasion, Christopher Biggins farted during the episode's countdown and reduced himself and the cue-awaiting cast to naughty hysterical laughter — they could hardly speak! Molly Weir had tears cascading down her silver-painted face. Sue Nicholls, fully expecting a retake, mimed to her off-camera dresser, while Michael Staniforth guffawed through his lines.

The scene ended. I jumped up from my director's chair yelling, "I'm going down to the floor to murder them!"

As I stormed through the adjacent room of lighting and rack operatives, I noticed they were all laughing.

"What's so funny?" I asked.

The lighting director answered. "*That* was. We don't know what they were all laughing at but, whatever it was, it made us all laugh too."

I headed back to my chair. If it made that lot laugh, the audience would as well.

One of *Rentaghost*'s most popular characters was Dobbin, introduced in our Christmas special *Rentasanta*, when Mr Claypole made a pantomime horse come alive. We rented in an existing skin plus head. I was amazed to discover that the grinning horse face had a wonderful personality on camera. John Asquith and Wiliam Perrie, sweating inside the costume as front and back, soon made Dobbin into a vivid, adorable character.

After one series, the head got bashed about a bit and so a replacement was manufactured. But something was wrong — it was finely crafted but Dobbin wasn't loveable any more. I said to the designer, "Nice as the new head is, it hasn't got the same expression."

"But the old head is disintegrating!"

I said, quite firmly, that we needed to re-integrate it.

And so we did. Dobbin was a true one-off.

One time, we were filming near a junior school and the kids were very excited to learn that *Rentaghost* was in the vicinity. A teacher asked, "Is Dobbin there?"

I said, "Well, he *might* be."

I liaised with the teachers for a school assembly to be held. At its height, the doors burst open at the back of the hall and Dobbin galloped down the aisle. The kids went wild.

That was lessons out of the window for the rest of the day.

* * *

Back to Granada and the hooting of the car horn outside the room where we were celebrating the sixth birthday of *Coronation Street*. I got a message to go to the parked car. It was Vanya doing a runner from the penthouse. In Don's car — with as much booty crammed in as possible. Pots, pans, linen, cutlery, plates, washing-up liquid, boxes and her entire wardrobe.

"What's all this?"

"What do you think it is? Hop in — I'll give you a lift to London. I left your room OK."

I accepted the offer, removing the egg cups from the passenger seat. I had intended to later get a train to the capital to stay with my friends the Clarkes in Kensington. Sunny Clarke was the sister of Maureen Halligan, with whom I had worked in theatre in Dublin. They were related to the great Irish artist, Harry Clarke. Their father was Michael Clarke, the actor.

Vanya drove off like a maniac, en route to her house in Chelsea. We got lost in Edgbaston, which she thought must be Chiswick — far from it. I sat quietly while she tiraded about what a rat Don was. I got quieter and wished she'd concentrate on the road.

After a perilous encounter with a truck near Reading, we eventually drove into London and screeched to a rattling halt in Richard's Place, Chelsea. A gentleman was waiting for Vanya at her home — old friend Maurice Binder, who had created all the James Bond title sequences. He was going to help her unload. I left them to it.

A smouldering admirer of Vanya's was lurking in the shadows opposite the house — a famous cello player. He wasn't playing the cello then, just jealously watching Vanya's abode for other suspected *innamoratos*.

My leaving the house made me a good target.

He hopped on a motorbike and revved after me, with the intention of smashing me to bits against the walls of the Chelsea terraces. Nimble on foot, I avoided him as he collided with a dustbin. I hopped into a taxi to

Kensington Park Gardens.

"What time do you call this?" demanded Sunny Clarke.

"Half past twelve — midnight."

She pulled the sofa away from the wall and the mattress flopped down. Such was my accommodation with the wonderful Clarkes — Sunny, and her children, Ann, Michelle, Sunniva and Michael. A bit of an uneasy weekend in London followed, then a train back to Manchester on Sunday night to an empty penthouse — very empty. Don rang from Tangiers or somewhere.

"Hi, Don, how was the shoot?"

"Fabulous." They always are. "I'll be back on Tuesday evening and Chris Kelly, the reporter, will have a bite to eat before he goes back home to Altrincham. Is that OK?"

"Vanya's gone."

"Ah. Will you be able to get a bite ready for us?" He was obviously prostrate with grief at the loss of Vanya. "See you Tuesday, about seven."

* * *

On Monday I was back on 'The Street', as we used to call it. A dynamic new director was in charge. His episode was set to reintroduce a very popular character. "It's curious that it never rains on the street," he declared.

"Of course it doesn't, you daft bugger," exclaimed Margot Bryant. "We do it in the studio!" Margot, who played Minnie Caldwell, was the reigning queen that week as Violet Carson was on holiday in Lytham St Annes — which is posh-speak for Blackpool.

"Rain would be good," mused the director. "I like rain."

On Tuesday, I had the afternoon off to prepare for Don's return. I went to Kendal Milnes' shop in Deansgate with a list. And to a butcher's.

The travellers returned that night. Don seemed unaware of the depleted home. I cooked steaks in a pan (new) and boiled potatoes in a saucepan (new) and produced a salad in a bowl (new) followed by ice cream and served the lot on assorted crockery (new) with smart cutlery (new). Don and Chris tucked and quaffed wine from elegant glasses (new). Chris went home. Don said:

"Well, that was OK, Jeremy. I'd better give you some cash. How much?"

"Three hundred and fifty pounds!"

His Moroccan tan faded. "What for?"

I gave him the list of purchases from Kendal Milnes, and the butcher's bill. Off he went to sleep in his room, with a laid-back outback attitude.

It was back to work the next day, with the rain-obsessed dynamic director. Of course, he got his wish — directors are gods.

For the recording day, sprinklers, hoses and plumbing were installed in the studio. I cued a scene in the Rovers Return. The scripted lines climaxed for the final scene.

"Guess who I saw heading back to Weatherfield?"

"Who?"

"Never!"

"She's never come back!"

"She is!"

I signalled the operatives to turn wheels, open sluices of water and send a positive Niagara fall down onto the rubber cobbled street. The torrent lashed from above, running into inadequate drains with a few sparks — we were dicing with death! Then came the next cue, for an actress in a white-belted trenchcoat with an umbrella to come round the corner. On the next cue, she hit her mark, by now, washed away in the torrent. Somehow she found it — again, such a pro! She lifted the umbrella and the camera zoomed in to show Pat Phoenix as Elsie Tanner in close-up, returning to Coronation Street — her face glistening, a sardonic smile on her crimsoned lips, her brilliant eyes turned upward.

Roll credits. Fabulous stuff!

It took a week to dry out the studio. We moved to another — luckily Sydney Bernstein had plenty. The dynamic director moved to Hollywood.

The next day, Don said that he'd run into Vanya on her way to read the news. "How was she?" I asked.

"OK."

He was lucky she hadn't stabbed him with one of the stolen knives.

Don and I settled into an *Odd Couple* relationship. I got the urge to go to the BBC in London and I could stay in Kensington Park Gardens with the Clarkes. Deansgate was quite posh but Kensington was posher — and near the BBC.

I lived very happily with Sunny and her children when I first came to London. Her sister Maureen and her family were my best friends. I had experienced homesickness away from Ireland but the Irishness of the Clarkes made up for that.

Scene 5

You can always switch it off

Auntie. The BBC. The DG-dom of information, entertainment and adoration of the British Public. An institution of such intrigue and shenaniganism that it made the Florentine court of the Borgias look like Toytown.

I got the job as a Holiday Relief Assistant Floor Manager, or AFM, in Drama Series. I'd been receiving £19 a week in Granada. The BBC paid me £15 10 shillings a week. No matter — I was there! I was to work on a series called *Witch Hunt*. Very exciting. My bosses were two girls. Fiona Cumming was the PA — what we called Floor Manager — as I'd been in Granada; the other was Shirley Coward, the production secretary. She later became a highly experienced vision mixer, who I worked with often.

I discovered that the role of the AFM in Drama Series was a sort of glorified props man and dogsbody — "Prompt, Jeremy!" *Witch Hunt* was recorded at Riverside Studios in Hammersmith, after filming locations in Gloucestershire. Important props included waxen dolls impaled with nails — the show wasn't called *Witch Hunt* for nothing! These sinister statuettes were crucial to the plot, so I diligently protected them.

"What are those things in a shoe box at the end of your bed, Jeremy?" declared my landlady, Sunny Clarke, one morning.

"What things?"

"I'm going straight to the priest. You're obviously up to something dodgy!"

She was a fervent Roman Catholic.

It took a lot of inadequate explanations going down the road of props and a firm denial that I wasn't up to creepy black magic.

The director of *Witch Hunt* was a bossy Scot. "There's a lot of film on this show, Jeremy. Can you tell me if you have any experience in that direction?"

"Yes. The last film I worked on was *The Spy Who Came in from the Cold*. What was yours?"

Touché.

We got on well after that. He kept wanting to talk about Elizabeth Taylor.

The next show I was scheduled on was *Pride and Prejudice*. Two demented lesbians were in charge, shouting and yelling in an office down the corridor.

"I can't work on that," I said to Shaun Sutton, the Head of Department.

He was very understanding, in a BBC sort of way. "I can get a job at ATV in Birmingham," I said.

"No need, Jeremy." Nobody ever had to leave the BBC — it had a Jesuit mantra. "I'll arrange a transfer for you to Studio Management."

He did. I got a job on the news at Alexandra Palace.

I thought that Alexandra Palace was near Buckingham Palace. It wasn't. it was miles away from Kensington Park Gardens. Endless travelling! I arrived late on my first day.

"You missed the 1.30 bulletin!" an irate Australian news editor bellowed at me.

"No, I didn't! I saw it in a shop window in Wood Green, trying to find this bloody place!"

All the floor managers had to do on the news was drop their right hand under the camera lens to let the newscaster know he was on the air. Michael Aspel was my favourite. When I announced "five seconds!" he'd sing under the titles. "*You'll wonder where the yellow went, when you brush your teeth with Pepsodent!* Hello, here is the news. 2,000 people were killed today in Vietnam..."

My least favourite newscaster was a sour-faced national idol whom I won't name. I'd noticed he only had little stubby pencils to mark his scripts so — by way of ingratiating arse-licking — I left a batch of new pencils on his desk.

"What are these?" he thundered.

"New pencils. You only have little stubby ones."

He swept the pencils off the desk.

"Little stubby pencils don't stick up."

"Stick up where?" I quaked.

"Up in front of my tie when I am reading the news!"

Dear God, I thought. Is this what I trained at the Brendan Smith Academy of Acting for?

* * *

When I'd been at RTÉ, I was sent to work for a BBC producer on loan — Patricia Foy. I was last on the list of floor managers assigned to her. She'd been getting through floor managers at the rate of knots. Luckily, she liked me, and we became lifelong friends. Her programmes were big classical music shows, featuring the RTÉ National Symphony Orchestra playing ballet and operatic gems, conducted by Tibor Paul.

The great soprano Montserrat Caballé was scheduled to let rip with *Vissi d'arte* from *Tosca*. A huge set was designed for Scarpia's study, where the heroine was to sing her heartfelt aria; a suitably glowering extra was booked to menace as Scarpia — it was going to be great stuff!

At the planning meeting beforehand, Miss Foy patiently explained the complexities of shooting the piece.

There was an interruption. A somewhat ditsy secretary put her head around the door and announced, "Mrs Cable can't come," and withdrew.

No one had ever heard of Mrs Cable, so the statement was ignored. Our diva Caballé was to arrive in Dublin from Barcelona the following day.

She didn't.

A nervous call to her agent in Paris confirmed she wasn't coming. With Agatha Christie cunning, I worked out the ominous meaning of "Mrs Cable can't come" — it was obviously an Irish mistranslation!

Miss Foy was hopping mad. Another soprano had to be booked. Norma Burrowes was found — her brother Wesley wrote for RTÉ's soap opera

The Riordans, so maybe a bit of family connection was involved. Miss Burrowes was agreeable. Great! Then came a grave mistake. Miss Burrowes asked what Caballé was to have sung. Paddy Foy, an agreeable negotiator, rashly told her, "*Visi d'arte* from *Tosca*."

"Terrific!" declared La Burroughs. "I'll sing *The Jewel Song* from *Faust*, as Marguerite."

Rats! For context, *The Jewel Song* takes place in a forest at a tree stump.

So Scarpia's study had to be turned into a sylvan glade. And there were props too — jewels. The props department supplied a suitable casket, unfortunately crammed with poppets — plastic beads that did just that, plus other tawdry glitter. Our Marguerite was having none of that tat.

I raided my landlady's jewel box to supply suitable opulence. I was lodging in Greenfield Manor, across the road from RTÉ. Shelah Richards was agreeable to the loan of her valuables. She understood the necessity of drama, having been the original Nora in Sean O'Casey's *The Plough and the Stars* at the Abbey Theatre in 1926. Shelah became a TV director — working on *The Riordans* — and my best-ever landlady, who greatly enriched my life.

***

Where was I? Back to BBC News and working in Studio Management. Apart from the thrill of news, I was relegated to other departments, including Music and Arts, where a great pal, and now my BBC advocate, Paddy Foy was a producer of lofty music programmes — and I mean *lofty*. She did gala performance ballet shows with her friend Margot Fonteyn and Margot's friend Rudolf Nureyev. Paddy also worked with huge opera stars like the American Jessye Norman and directed the BBC's *Music For You* show with Eric Robinson.

Paddy was married to Richard (Dick) Levin, the BBC's first Head of Design; he had also designed the Festival of Britain. They lived in a big house in Barnes, with a toucan, two cockatoos and Coco, an African grey parrot. There were some small aggressive dogs about too.

Paddy asked me to dine there a lot because she thought I was getting too skinny. When I was sent to work with her, we didn't do any work. I now discovered that the BBC was not what you knew but *who* you knew.

My friendship with Dick and Paddy elevated me to an eye-flicker of recognition from some senior management egos and heads of other departments — apart from Studio Management, who adored Paddy and were terrified of Dick!

A Jackanory *closing credit card for* Green Smoke *from 1969*

Scene 6

'Jackanory, Jackanory...'

Studio Management told me to report to Children's Programmes to be the AFM on *Jackanory*, a storytelling programme, featuring popular stars reading popular books, punctuated by picture captions illustrating the stories. A great format, devised by Joy Whitby, who had also come up with *Play School*. Mrs Whitby was defecting from the BBC to London Weekend Television on the day I turned up to work on Jackanory at Kensington House behind Shepherd's Bush. I reported to Reception and was directed to the Fourth Floor. I got into the lift when a commanding voice rang out.

"Hold the lift!"

The most glamorous lady got in, clutching every newspaper published that day. She was tall, blonde with hair swirled around, blue eyeshadow, great figure, classy high heels.

"Push four!"

"I have!"

Then all the newspapers slithered from her grasp. I picked them up while she put her back into stalling the lift on the fourth floor.

"I'll carry the papers for you."

"Who are you?"

"I'm Jeremy — I'm the *Jackanory* AFM."

She flung open a door at the end of the corridor. I followed with the papers. It was like a Māori long hut, with loads of people working hard.

"Everyone — this is Jeremy!" she announced.

I detected a quaver of terror as they bleated, "Hello, Jeremy." It was the same element of fear I detected when she entered the office.

I asked her where *Jackanory* was. "On the other side of the building."

I thanked her and she wished me well. All very courteous. "What a nice lady," I thought. The office door said '*Blue Peter* — Editor Biddy Baxter'.

There was a fight in progress on the *Jackanory* side of the building.

Two guys were yelling at each other and swinging punches — the secretaries swooned in terror. A record player was blaring out *A Whiter Shade of Pale* by Procol Harum. I retreated into a poky office, which had 'AFMs — *Play School* and *Jackanory*' inscribed on the door. Inside was a smouldering unworking actress who was the *Play School* AFM.

"They are all as mad as rats here," she informed me, dragging on her cigarette. "*Play School* is madder than *Jackanory*! I'll take you down to the rehearsal in Lime Grove studios to see how the joint kicks in."

"Are they near — the studios?"

"We'll take a Project Number cab. Project Number cabs are the perk of the job." They certainly were — you could go anywhere, ordering through the Transport Department and giving them a project number.

We left the corridors with the guys still slogging away, while others helped the defecting Mrs Joy Whitby into a cab laden with her goods and chattels, bound for the new London Weekend Television studios.

Procol Harum was still blaring out.

The Lime Grove Studios were two minutes away in the Project Number cab. The cab expense was justified by my new friend carrying props for *Play School* in a very small bag.

The *Play School* dress rehearsal was in full swing. Two actors were presenting, Phyllida Law and Lee Montague. She was the mother of Dame Emma Thompson and the wife of Eric Thompson, who narrated *The Magic Roundabout*. Lee Montague had read the first ever *Jackanory*.

They were about to launch into the *Play School* song.

"Would you like to hear a song?" Miss Law coyly asked the camera.

'JACKANORY, JACKANORY...'

Presenters loved asking questions to the camera and then immediately answering them. "Then you will!"

Off went Jonathan Cohen on the piano. Miss Law sang, "I went knick-knack up against the tree, up against the tree, up against the tree. I went knick-knack up against the tree — early in the morning!"

Mr Montague then sang, "I went knick-knack up against the wall, up against the wall, up against the wall. I went knick-knack up against the wall — early in the morning."

Miss Law trilled in. "I went knick-knack up against the door, up against the door, up against the door. I went knick-knack up against the door — early in the morning!"

When Lee Montague started knick-knacking up against the chair, I noticed one of the cameramen shuddering with laughter. The amusement caught on like a plague, as the presenters knick-knacked all over the place. They were fully aware of the risqué hilarity they were causing.

At the end of the interminable song, the director could be plaintively heard through the earphones.

"Come on, studio. Share the joke!"

*　*　*

'Jackanory, Jackanory...' That was the welcome uttered by David Coulter on the signature tune, only to be replaced by John Prowse when David defected to LWT, following Joy Whitby.

My first job on *Jackanory* was marking up the captions for the story narratives and operating the kaleidoscope — a device that the camera pointed at as it whirled around. This had been invented by the Visual Effects department, a set-up which had the resources to blast us all to smithereens, should they choose. Ever since working with them, I have approached any upright piano with trepidation.

Eventually, I was interviewed to become a director of *Jackanory*.

"What story would you choose?"

"*Hiawatha*."

"And who would you ask to tell the story of *Hiawatha*?"

"Dame Sybil Thorndike, as the 'wrinkled old Nokomis, daughter of the Moon'."

"And what makes you think that Dame Sybil would tell the story?"

"She'd love to — I asked her at dinner last night."

I'd been out with Glynis Casson, Dame Sybil's granddaughter.

Clinched! I got the job as director of *Jackanory*. *Hiawatha* went away. He'd served his purpose.

As the director of *Jackanory*, I had to write five 15-minute scripts. Books were carved up to fill these slots — we called it 'adapting'. Once adapted you punctuated the scripts with illustrations called captions. Then you directed in the studio. The captions were a strategic device for editing the shows. If the narrator had a hiccup in the narration you just re-recorded the section in between the captions. You had to come up with a set in which to present the story. So, a set designer was on board. Then the casting — this was a doddle. Famous actors were chomping at the bit to present *Jackanory* — all they had to do was to read the autocue and display their unique talents. They had rehearsed in our offices beforehand, mainly for timing the shows.

My first show was *Witches*, presented by Rosemary Leach. I used the music of *Mars, the Bringer of War* by Holst. Anna Home, the boss, said it would scare the pants off the kids — so we switched to a bit of Tchaikovsky. From there, I nervously moved on to other shows. I loved Anna Home. She was dubious about me, but she knew that I had something to offer.

For *The Magic Pudding*, I wanted Barry Humphries to read it, dressed as a wombat. That was shot down, so another Australian, Rod McLennan presented it, with great aplomb. I worked with the great Ted Ray, who read *Thomas the Tank Engine*, long before Ringo Starr became the voice of the books on TV. Another triumph was Su Pollard, who read *Flaming Flamingos and Raging Robots* by Margaret Mahy. Su was both a flaming flamingo and raging robot — and a big hit with the kids.

Then along came Thora Hird to read *Mrs Pepperpot*. The set was a leafy tree, under which Dame Thora sat on a bench wearing her best summer frock (the presenters usually supplied their own costume) and a big wig (presenters, if necessary, wore their own wigs too). We were about to start the rehearsal of the opening episode when the control room — where I was controlling — suddenly filled up with Very Important Guests of the Director-General, wanting to see television in the making. The only television being made that morning was *Jackanory*'s *Mrs Pepperpot*. They all hoped to see *The Onedin Line* but — that's showbusiness.

'JACKANORY, JACKANORY...'

There was some technical glitch, so we had to stop and start. Thora's opening line was: "Hello! Do you know Mrs Pepperpot? You don't? Well, she was a little woman who shrank to the size of a pepperpot at the most inconvenient moments..."

The technical hitch forced Dame Thora to keep repeating the opening lines. She was getting a bit beady. The DG's guests watched intensely — they were enjoying all the creative tension. OK. Everything fixed, we started again. The signature tune played over the kaleidoscope — *'Jackanory, Jackanory'*, then we dissolved to Dame Thora on the bench. The camera tracked in. Dame Thora glinted into the lens.

"Hello! Do you know Mrs Pepperpot? You don't? Well, sod *off!*"

* * *

The artists who painted the pictures for *Jackanory* were a talented bunch. The Children's Graphic Department was headed by Hilary Hayton. She and Mina Martinez, Paul Birkbeck, Graham McCallum and Laurence Henry did the illustrations for *Play School* and *Jackanory*. Outside geniuses were also recruited — the likes of Quentin Blake, Jan Brychta, Gareth Floyd, Julek Heller, Jan Pieńkowski and Richard Kennedy. All wonderful artists. *Jackanory* was a tall order. At least 60 pictures were needed for each week's worth of programmes. Whatever happened to all those beautifully executed paintings? Well, I have a few. So does Anna, along with Angela Beeching, who became the show's producer. She has hundreds stashed under her spare bed.

Anna Home gave me a book to adapt — *The Land of Green Ginger* — a sort of sequel to *Aladdin* by American writer Noel Langley, originally published in 1938. How Mr Langley knew that The Land of Green Ginger was a street in Hull, was a mystery. Or did he know at all? He had also been a screenwriter on MGM's *The Wizard of Oz*, starring Judy Garland.

If any Friends of Dorothy thought that *The Wizard of Oz* was camp, then by jingo — read *The Land of Green Ginger*! It was full of funny innuendo, strange voices and magic. But who was to perform it? Anna and I racked our brains and combed through *Spotlight*, the actors' directory.

In my bedsit in Vicarage Gate, I used to listen to *Round the Horne* on the radio — a hilarious show. The most hilarious star in it was Kenneth Williams, so perfect and right for *The Land of Green Ginger*. Anna agreed, so I rang his agent, Peter Eade, and made the offer.

Mr Eade doubted that Kenneth Williams would be interested, so I made a big pitch of how the children would love him and that Mr Williams would have a fun time, *et cetera*. I mentioned that I was a friend of Siobhán McKenna. Kenneth had been the Dauphan to her *Saint Joan* during the London run.

That clinched it.

The bait was being sniffed. It then went a bit wobbly because Hattie Jacques had fibbed to him. "You realise you have to wear a big hat that lights up with *Jackanory* in neon on the top?"

The dissuasion that followed got Kenneth to agree to do the show and enabled me to get him into a kaftan. He moaned that he looked like Beatrice Lillie. But our rocky path to the studio was evened out by Kenneth falling in love with Jonathan Cohen, who was playing the music for the episodes. Kenneth's narration was magnificent and the audience loved him — particularly when he leaned into the camera at the end of the episodes and announced emphatically, "Good-*bye*!"

Kenneth became the second-best most popular presenter on *Jackanory*. The first-best most popular presenter was Bernard Cribbins. The last *Jackanory* I directed Kenneth in was *James and the Giant Peach*. By then, he had become a dear and hilarious friend.

Another *Jackanory* hit featured Dame Judi Dench reading Beatrix Potter's *The Tailor of Gloucester*. Judi had done *Jackanory* before and had the performance technique down to a fine art. She used to get into a huddle with the autocue operator and go through the script in detail — underlining and highlighting every word. The autocue operators had to establish the closest rapport with the presenter, rolling the printed dialogue in perfect coordination with the artist's performance.

Another star who entered my galaxy through *Jackanory* was Elaine Stritch, reading *Charlie and the Great Glass Elevator* by Roald Dahl, a firm favourite author with children. Elaine had all the ingredients of a great Broadway Star: A filthy temper, a drink problem, a mean-spirited disposition — and an enormous talent. She lived in London's Savoy Hotel with an illegal immigrant — her dachshund, Bridget.

Elaine's residency at The Savoy was secured by plugging the hotel on every chat show she appeared. "Before you ask me any questions, Russell (or Terry or Melvyn Bragg), let me tell you that I am living in the BEST

HOTEL IN THE WORLD — The Savoy!"

Well, that guaranteed free digs.

For *Jackanory*, Elaine wore a wonderful navy-blue suede trouser suit, designed by Janet Ibbotson. She told me that her fee had paid for the matching little hat that she didn't wear on camera. I doubted that she had paid for the suit. Couture exposure on TV was always a couture boost.

On the second day of recording *Charlie and the Great Glass Elevator*, Elaine hadn't turned up when were due to start. I filled in with caption rehearsals. Finally, the floor manager, Clair Dean, informed me that our star had arrived at reception.

"Tell her I'm hopping mad!"

I could hear the flurry of Elaine's arrival in the studio. Then Clair told me that I was to shut my eyes in the control room. I complied and could hear a lot of shuffling, laughs and moving of cameras on the studio floor.

"You are to open your eyes now, Jeremy," said Clair.

There, on the monitors, in a big close-up, was Bridget the dachshund, wearing a bandana on her head, sitting in Elaine's chair, behind which the diva herself was hiding, speaking in canine tones.

"Hi, Jeremy, Bridget here, saying I'm very sorry for delaying that naughty Elaine. I had to have a *wee-wee* in Shepherds Bush!"

Of course, Elaine did a terrific job on the show and we got on famously. At one point, during a break in the recordings, Elaine asked if my PA, Maria Ball, could come down for a word. Mystified, Maria left the control room and went down to the floor. I instructed the boom operator to eavesdrop on the word Miss Stritch wanted with Maria.

Elaine whispered, "Hi, Maria. Good to see you. Could you do me a big favour? I've got the curse real bad. Could you pop round to the off-licence and get me a small bottle of brandy? I'm sure you can charge it to the programme."

Maria ran the errand, mortified by the star's complaint and the prospect of having to visit an off-licence mid-afternoon in Shepherd's Bush.

A couple of months later, I was seconded to direct a show for the BBC Drama department, which was to re-introduce Russell Harty to the BBC after a defection to ITV. The programme was to feature Elaine Stritch, Penelope Keith, Alan Bennett and Russell, a quartet. It was called *Quartet* — a sort of revue featuring the stars singing and reading. I called it *Star Wars*! The producer was Alan Shallcross. I suspected that Elaine and Penny

— a dear friend — had requested me as director.

Alan Shallcross asked me to accompany him to Alan Bennett's house to rehearse Mr Bennett. A Project Number taxi dropped us near Chalk Farm. In the small drive of Alan Bennett's house, an old van was wedged. Alan Shallcross and I squeezed past it to get to the front door. From inside the van came yelling and banging and expletives.

"What's that?" I nervously asked.

"Don't ask," replied Alan and rang the bell.

Mr Bennett opened the door and received us, graciously, in a panelled room. We rehearsed and went past the van on the way out — to more effing and blinding. I didn't ask, having been told not to by Alan. It was the Lady in the Van, later played by Maggie Smith in the film of the same name, written by Alan Bennett.

The couturier Jean Muir was to supply the dresses for Penny and Elaine for the show, but good ol' Elaine wasn't having that. Oh, no — she got two young men to run her up a somewhat alarming apparel and duly credited the boys during her warm-up.

The audience for the show was the BBC Board of Governors and their respective partners. As the clock counted down to the start of recording, I swiftly instructed the floor manager to remove a large bag that Elaine had shoved under her chair. Aesthetically, it was mucking up the opening shot of the four silhouetted seated stars and I creepily suspected that it contained Elaine's insulin needle. She'd recently been diagnosed with diabetes and there was every possibility that she would start shooting up during Penny's solo to camera. As the musical intro began, I spotted Elaine looking under her chair, aware of being thwarted.

When the time came for her to return to America, Elaine invited her agent Michael Whitehall to The Savoy to say goodbye. He was confronted by two huge, wrapped parcels.

"These are presents, Michael," she effused. "For you and your darling wife, Hilary. To say a big thank you for looking after me in London. No, no, don't open them here! Open them at home — both of you — with my love. Thank you, thank you."

Michael got a taxi home to Putney, carrying the enormous presents. Later, he and his wife tore open the parcels. They contained towelling dressing gowns, slippers, towels, face flannels and soaps, scents and shampoos — all emblazoned with the legend 'The Savoy Hotel'!

Filming The Mix, *directed by Andrew Morgan, starring his wife Jacki and a starkers me*

Scene 7

Par for the course

Back to *Jackanory* — churning it out. I started to get a bit twitchy. I went to my boss, Monica Sims: "I'm getting a bit twitchy on *Jackanory*."

"No need for twitchy, Jeremy." I detected her raising her eyes to Heaven — and then, a mental rummage. "I'll send you on a course!"

"What sort of course? Flower arranging? Cookery? Carpentry? Anything!"

"Don't be ridiculous! An advanced film direction course."

"I've been on advanced film! *Witch Hunt*! *The Spy Who Came in from the Cold... Enter Inspector Duval* at Ardmore Studios, starring Anton Diffring, directed by a sex maniac — what more?"

"The BBC Advanced Film Direction Course would be very good for you," she said crisply. "I'm putting your name down!"

The BBC Advanced Film Direction Course was a bit plonky. A crowd of us gathered — refugees from Religious Programmes, Documentaries and Drama. The course was run by Charles Castle, an ex-tango dancer from

South Africa, and Hannen Foss, an accomplished film cameraman who worked for various departments within the BBC. They didn't get on.

There was a row on the first day, as they entered the room where we were all sitting.

"I'll go in first."

"No, you won't — I will."

"Get out of my way!"

"No, I *won't!*"

So they both jammed against each other in the entrance. All our eyes were swivelling. The course runners were wedged in the doorway. Charles Castle was wearing a shirt that he'd obviously saved from his tango-dancing days. Mr Foss was in a suit and tie.

They proceeded to lecture us about advanced film direction in a kind of double act. I quickly realised that they were talking through their arses but I was, nonetheless, courteously attentive.

Sitting on either side of me were Andrew Morgan, a Drama PA, and Janie Grace, a mate from Children's Programmes. The mates in Children's Programmes were good mates. There was Marilyn Fox, Angela Beeching and Paul Stone, plus Anna on the *Jackanory* front. Our Head of Department was Monica Sims, and the Deputy Head was Edward Barnes, who used to be Paddy Foy's PA on *Music For You*. The Manager of Children's Programmes was George Ageros who, as a sound mixer, had also worked on Paddy's operatic triumphs.

So, you see, the BBC was one happy deranged family.

Andrew Morgan was the salt of the earth. He looked like a handsome rugby player and was ambitious. Actually, they were all avidly ambitious. I was a bit *seen-it, done-it*. Andrew became an *objet de désir* for our tutor, Charles Castle. That left us all in huge giggles and gave Andrew the heebie-jeebies as the hopeless pursuit progressed.

The Advanced Film Direction Course couldn't advance quickly enough for me. The grand finale was to be the making and showing of the advanced films which we had all directed. You were given half a day to shoot a subject of your own devising, then cobble it together with suitable noise — otherwise known as editing and dubbing.

With enormous cunning, I figured out that if I volunteered to film first, I'd have nearly a fortnight off while the others slogged away. Maybe I could even take a holiday? I rashly confided these vacational plans to my course colleagues. "We'll fix him!" they muttered darkly, as they toiled at the scripts of the final exercises, obviously livid that they hadn't come up with such a scheme themselves!

Charles Castle sought me out: "Because you will have spare time after your final exercise, we have decided that you will appear in all the other films — cameos, bit parts, here and there."

Rats! *Thwarted!*

I shot my film, in which a young Victorian girl was pursued by a gorilla in Chiswick Park, to the music of *Les Patineurs* by Meyerbeer. I thought it would be ahead of its time. The other directors of the course were more ambitious.

Andrew had come up with a gritty drama to be shot in half a day. In his story, a driver was to deliver a consignment of cement in a huge rolling mixer on a truck. He decided to call on his wife in his truck. A big mistake — she was *in flagrante* with another man when the guy called. He saw the scene. In revenge, he opened the bonnet of the car parked outside their house, tilted the entire consignment of cement into the engine of the car, and drove off. The lover then came out of the house, hopped on a bicycle and rode away. A vicar emerged from the house next door and looked, in horror, at his car oozing cement.

Good stuff, Andrew!

I was playing the lover, with Andrew's wife Jacki as the cement driver's spouse. Andrew said I was the only man he trusted to be naked in bed with his wife.

All the finished films were to be shown at a screening, attended by the respective heads of departments. Monica Sims couldn't come. She was having her hair done. Edward Barnes said that he would rather have red hot needles driven into his feet. A similar sentiment was expressed by Anna Home, though not so vividly. But the Heads of Drama, Documentaries and Religion did turn up.

The Drama Heads were very impressed with their PA's efforts. At the do afterwards, I heard them enthuse that the PAs would make wonderful directors in the department — but only if they resigned from the BBC and became freelance!

Their tone was wheedling and persuasive. This was very dangerous — no pension, no permanency, no BBC job. Several snaffled the lethal bait, including Andrew Morgan, who became a very famous freelance director.

ITV's *Heartbeat* was one of his big hits. "It will run forever!" he said.

It didn't.

The perils of freelancing. Later on, Andrew summoned me to help unpick the complexities of blue screen broomstick flying on *The Worst Witch*.

Back I went to *Jackanory*. My department mates returned from the studio one day. "We all saw you on the monitors during camera line-up," they announced cheerily.

"How exciting! Was it an early Ardmore film? Me, as an extra?"

"No, you were starkers, hopping out of a woman's bed!"

Dear God — Andrew's film was being shown to the Drama bosses!

Scene 8

In Dublin's fair city...

News came from The Emerald Isle that my friend Lelia Doolan had become the new Head of Light Entertainment at RTÉ. I visualised a smart career move for myself with the nostalgic opportunity to see my parents, my granny and Nigel, Naomi, Jacqui and Giselle and aunts Sheila and Carmel Leahy, and Lona Moran and Shelah Richards in Greenfield Manor. A job was offered — producer in Light Entertainment in RTÉ. It was going to take a while to move from London and issue my sad farewell to Children's Programmes and the BBC.

My grandmother often posted the Irish newspapers to my address in Vicarage Gate. The Dublin *Evening Herald* arrived with a note: "This should interest you! Love Nana." The headline report was about a revolution in RTÉ! Led by Lelia Doolan! Who had then resigned! Jesus! My notice had already been given to the BBC and Vicarage Gate! My bags were packed!

So, I went straight to the top and rang Tom Hardiman, the Director-

General, who I fortunately knew from when he was Head of Engineering. He was calmly reassuring, despite my panic and said I'd be welcome back to RTÉ. The new Head of Light Entertainment was Adrian Cronin, with whom I had toured Europe in *Saint Joan*. He had played the Page who spots the kingfisher, which was a better part than the Dauphin's Page. But no theatrical rivalry — we were good friends, luckily!

Adrian was to be my new boss. When I turned up at RTÉ there was only a secretary in the Light Entertainment department, Maura Cassidy.

"Where's everyone?"

"You just missed them. Go and catch up with them. At the airport"

"What are they doing at the airport?"

"They've gone to welcome back Dana."

"What's Dana?"

"Dana! She won the Eurovision Song Contest!"

Of course, she did. Dana only needs one name to be a star.

Maura drove me to the airport. There was a swift reunion and hellos with my new colleagues before a plane landed with 'DANA' painted in huge letters on the flank. A little orchestra ran out onto the runway and assembled at the bottom of the plane's steps. It was a huge honour for Ireland to win the Eurovision Song Contest. It still is! The airport was ablaze with excitement. Vital flight announcements were curtailed. Not-in-the-know departing passengers panicked, thinking war had been declared.

The orchestra struck up. Dana appeared in the plane's doorway to immense cheers and launched into the winning song.

"*All kinds of everything...*" rang out on all the announcement speakers at Dublin Airport. "*Remind me of you!*"

Ireland has always had a dotty charm for me — be it Mícheál Mac Liammóir walking down Grafton Street in full make-up or a woman in Ballymun discovering the face of Jesus on a pizza. Dana singing *All Kinds of Everything* from a plane at the airport was a moment of marvellous dottiness. But her triumph fell hollowly on the ears of the financial controllers of RTÉ, who would have to stage the competition next year at huge expense.

* * *

Time for a digression... During my previous existence at RTÉ, I was floor managing the Bolshoi Ballet for a series of programmes produced by

Patricia Foy; the Bolshoi were performing at the Gaiety Theatre at the time. The RTÉ Symphony Orchestra was to play for the Gaiety. The TV deal was clinched by this leverage: "No TV, no orchestra!" The negotiations were done through a woman ominously called Nina Deadman. She was the Bolshoi liaison officer and the KGB rep.

The great ballerina Maya Plisetskaya was to dance *The Swan* by Saint-Saëns. The studio lighting director magnificently illuminated a Monet-esque set of waterlilies, rippling water and dappled moonlight. The Prima Ballerina Assoluta waddled into the studio, took one look at the set and said, "*Niet!*"

What was there to 'niet' about it?

Huddled conversation followed between Plisetskaya and Mrs Deadman — a lot of 'niets' and arm flapping. We all waited. This would be sorted, we told ourselves, nervously. Eventually, it was.

The great dancer wanted a follow spot — a light to move with her — which would, of course, aesthetically screw up the set. But when she got it I understood why. On point, undulating her arms with her back to the camera, the follow spot worked as a handy mirror to guide her.

Mrs Deadman and I were in accord.

Jump forward three years to 1967. I'm working at *Jackanory* for the Beeb. An envelope arrived for me in the post. BBC directors had all their post opened for them by their secretaries in those days. I found everyone in the office huddled, looking at the envelope's contents.

"How did he get involved with people like *this*?"

"Remember Kim Philby, Burgess and Maclean!"

"What's in that envelope for me?"

It was an invitation from the Russian Ambassador, inviting me to a party at the Russian Embassy in Kensington Palace Gardens to celebrate the 50th anniversary of the Russian Revolution.

"You can't possibly go! Think of the poor Czar and Anastasia!"

"I won't and I will!"

And I did.

After all, Kensington Palace Gardens was just around the corner from my bedsit in Vicarage Gate. It would just be a little local social event. Truthfully, I don't know how I wangled the invitation. Could it have been Mrs Deadman? She wasn't at the party. Lots were. The only face I recognised was Dave Allen, the TV comedian. We didn't know one another. The Embassy was awash with vodka and great basins of caviar, dolloped out by beaming babushkas.

I fell in with a jolly bunch — the Third Secretary Lev Romanov and his wife, the Head of Overseas Scientific Technology and Head of Cultural Liaison, who knew my friend, Mrs Deadman. "A good comrade!" she said approvingly. My new friends were avidly interested in the BBC's recent conversion to colour. Dick Levin had told me that the BBC's understated colour template was based on the palette of Vermeer's paintings — rather than garish American and Japanese broadcasts.

The Russians and I arranged to meet on the roof garden of the Derry & Toms department store in Kensington the following Saturday.

Then I passed out, having lowered the vodka like Lucozade.

The bedsits in Vicarage Gate were electrified with the spectacle of me being carried up the stairs by a uniformed Russian chauffeur who then dumped me in my room.

Before we start hurling down a John le Carré scenario, you might ask, *why* was I asked along to this Russian hooley? Was I invited to be a lively addition — a party animal? Social or political? I could never work it out.

The following week, we met again on the roof garden of Derry & Tom's. The Russians angled for a visit to TV Centre but it wasn't on the cards; the arrival of the Third Secretary, the Head of Scientific Technology and the Head of Cultural Liaison would have created a diplomatic frisson which the BBC Visitor department didn't want. The Corporation was very wary of Russian infiltration after the Philby, Burgess and MacLean defections.

For me, this created a problem from an etiquette point of view. I wanted to reciprocate the hospitality I'd been shown when I passed out drunk at the Russians' festivities.

A solution occurred. I was assigned to be the AFM on a play — to be recorded in a theatre. The PA, Sue Stapely, asked me if I wanted any audience seats for the recording. Bingo!

"Actually, I do! Can I have six?"

"Six. That's good. Who for?"

"Friends in the Russian Embassy."

"You're not serious?"

"I am."

"Do you know the play we're working on?"

"What's that got to do with it?"

"A lot! It's *Chase Me Comrade!* starring Brian Rix — a farce about the defection of Rudolf Nureyev!"

Whoops! "Erm... they'll love the plot — they'll know the name! Send the tickets!"

The tickets came back. They knew the name. They didn't like the plot. Not long after that, my Embassy friends were all deported back to the Motherland as swaps for some espionage negotiation.

So that was the end of me and the Russians.

Well, not quite. I was to have an annual interview at the BBC. A ritual with my departmental manager to determine how I was getting along in the Corporation and to receive an increment, if deserved, in my pay packet. All went well until I noticed a Christmas tree logo stamped on my personnel file.

"What does that mean?" I asked, warily.

"Nothing."

I later discovered that Christmas trees stamped on your personnel file meant you were associated with the Russians and therefore viewed as a potential defector. But maybe that's just a BBC legend.

* * *

Back to before that last digression — when I was working in RTÉ's Light Entertainment department. I produced programmes that were sometimes light and sometimes entertaining. *A Handful of Songs* ticked the right boxes. It starred Anna McGoldrick and Danny Doyle, with the Pattersons as our house band and staging by Jo Cook, who I imported from *The Val Doonican Show* in London. The series was followed by the imaginatively titled *Another Handful of Songs* — this time starring Patricia Cahill, Dermot O'Brien and the Wolfe Tones.

RTÉ's reciprocal Eurovision Song Contest was looming. Auditions were held for song and singer — threatened by severe financial restraints and run along the lines of Mel Brook's *The Producers*.

"Too good — next!"

An unthinking comment I made that I thought the final choice was rather good was met with nervous eye-flickering. RTÉ was in tense talks with the European Broadcasting Union (EBU) ahead of the event. Some genius decided it would be wonderful to transport all the juries to Dublin for the broadcast. It was the sort of decision that made you think someone in the ranks had figured out how to really throw the shit in the fan!

As an RTÉ producer, I was to be the jury coordinator — a cat-herding job. Come the day, the Contest Gaiety Theatre and every hotel in Dublin within an asses' roar was crammed — with singers, EBU officials, bands, mothers, fathers, partners and juries. It was decreed that all the embassies in Dublin should throw a party to honour their musical representatives and jury members. This was actually a good money-saver. The embassies' countries would have to fork out for the hospitality!

Rehearsals thundered away at the Gaiety Theatre. The paint frame was designated as the jury room for the contest. Alas, it looked like the set for an Edgar Allen Poe novel. A guaranteed way to instil blind terror into visitors from dictator-manipulated states is to lock them in a dingy back room in an old theatre! TV monitors were installed to beam the contest to the jurors, bathing them in a creepy flicker.

The contest occurred. Monaco won — much to Ireland's relief — with a song titled like a toddlers' first-read book; *Un Banc, Un Arbre, Une Rue*, sung by Severine.

A big end-of-show party took place in Dublin Castle. As cabaret, a load of harpists plucked out traditional airs on the castle roof; the spectacle was glimpsed through the banqueting hall windows when the curtains swished back. The harpists wore chiffon cloaks, which billowed upwards in the warm night breeze. They sat on little platforms fastened to the castle's chimneys. It was a wonderful presentation — if vaguely suicidal.

RTÉ asked me to direct another Song Contest. How terrific! Where? Monaco? No. Castlebar in County Mayo. Equally spectacular, though not so cosmopolitan.

Monica Sims turned up in Dublin as the BBC representative at a European Conference about Children's Programmes. I took her to a variety show at the Gaiety — *Gaels of Laughter*, starring Ireland's Fanny Brice, the great Maureen Potter. I've never heard anyone enjoy themselves so much. Monica emitted gales of laughter at *Gaels*...

After the show, I took the Head of BBC Children's Programmes to the green room for an audience with the Emerald Isle's Queen of Comedy. A deep bonding followed. Monica was still laughing when I brought her back to the Royal Hibernian Hotel. Not long after, Maureen Potter was filming Patricia Lynch's *The Bookshop on the Quay* for *Jackanory*, directed by Marilyn Fox — a very talented, if somewhat nervous director. It was, appropriately, filmed in a bookshop on the Dublin Quays.

Marilyn went from Dublin to the Aran Islands to film an adaptation of *The Island of the Great Yellow Ox* by Walter Macken, a co-production between RTÉ and the BBC. Huge storms battered the Aran Islands. Marilyn managed to make a panic-stricken call to RTÉ. She said she was unable to get through to Anna Home, the BBC producer of the film, and asked if I could ring Anna to explain the communication problems.

I obliged. "Anna, Marilyn is in a frightful state and is unable to make any reports to you of the dreadful time she's having on the filming in the Aran Islands."

"What's the bad news?"

* * *

Gay Byrne, who presented *The Late Late Show* on RTÉ, wanted Kenneth Williams to appear on the programme as a guest. Could I arrange it? An agreeable phone call to Kenneth followed.

"I'll be arriving on Saturday at about nine."

"That's cutting it a bit fine, Kenneth, the show is on the air at ten."

"No, no, nine in the morning, nine in the morning! I want to see the city of Oscar Wilde! The city of Trinity College! The Book of Kells! The city of Yeats, Seán O'Casey, Joyce, Brendan Behan! Oh, it will be *fabulouso!*"

Early on the Saturday, I was taken to Dublin Airport by Jackie Dunn, one of RTÉ's regular drivers, in a smart car to collect Kenneth. He emerged from the plane, arm-in-arm with two Aer Lingus air hostesses who were falling about with laughter. We did the necessary tour and had a spot of lunch in the Shelbourne Hotel.

I had asked my landlady Shelah Richards if I could bring Kenneth to Greenfield Manor for tea and phoned Siobhán McKenna to ask her if she could be there as a surprise. Kenneth had been the Dauphin to her Saint Joan during the London run. I also invited journalist Emer O'Kelly, along with a photographer. Gay Byrne and his wife Kathleen would pop in for a drink. Greenfield Manor was across the road from RTÉ.

When we rumbled up the drive in the late afternoon, Shelah was waiting to greet us. A muddle caused her to expect Welsh character actor Hugh Williams — but that confusion was assuaged by Kenneth's great courtesy.

The great surprise was hiding behind a screen in the drawing room, jollying up for the reunion with a few tots of Cork Gin. And a glorious reunion it was — Kenneth's father used to cut Siobhán's hair for *Saint Joan* and they loved one another; not Siobhán and Kenneth's father, Kenneth and Siobhán.

A hilarious party followed, with Kenneth's wit in abundance. Gay sloped off to do *The Late Late Show* and Kathleen went home to watch. Later, Kenneth and I walked over to RTÉ, where I sat in the make-up room to watch the show. Kenneth rose above the dourness of the other guests magnificently and was great with Gay.

I received a call from my pals in the Olympia Theatre. They were watching the show and would I bring Kenneth to a party they were having that evening. Why not? The night was young and it was another opportunity to show Kenneth's further delights of Dublin. The delights were somewhat Rabelaisian but Kenneth had a whale of a time. He enjoyed huge flirtations with the stagehands of the Olympia, revelling in celebrity adulation.

In a somewhat tottery state, Jackie Dunn and I drove Kenneth back to the Montrose Hotel at an unspeakable hour. Next morning, he was as right as rain for the drive to Dublin Airport. He wrote me a letter about the wonderful time he'd had in Dublin — the party in Greenfield Manor with Shelah and Siobhán and how he loved Gay and Kathleen, and Emer.

It was, therefore, weird to read in Kenneth's diaries, published in 1993, after his death:

> "Thought a lot about the trip to Dublin. The atmosphere of *seediness* and decay about the city, and the feeling of utter provinciality combined to make me feel depressed."

Well, he certainly wasn't depressed at the hooley in the Olympia Theatre after *The Late Late Show*! But that was Kenneth. Like all of us, he had another inside — which was concealed by his outside. Gay asked him back to *The Late Late Show* again. No hesitation, no depression.

I've had dear friends who had ups and downs and Kenneth was certainly one of those. But I loved him, and he was very fond of me, for a long time.

Scene 9

'I have returned!'

Whoopee! Monica Sims had asked me to return to the BBC! My colleagues couldn't believe it. "We can't believe it — you're back!" declared Angela Beeching and Marilyn Fox.

A professional snag occurred.

Monica Sims was leaving Children's Programmes to become Controller of BBC Radio 4. My champion was to be replaced by Edward Barnes, who had been away on secondment to Hong Kong.

Heading my bets, I applied for a job as a producer in Light Entertainment and was interviewed by John Howard Davies — a lovely guy who I knew through Penny Keith, star of *The Good Life* and a friend of Wendy Duggan and her husband, Ron Riches.

Wendy was the animal supplier for BBC Children's Programmes — anything from a rat to an elephant. She was well-connected with London Zoo. Wendy and Ron lived in Putney with a flock of cockatoos and parrots and they threw very good parties.

It must be time for another digression. So, Ron and Wendy... In her days as a young beauty, Wendy had been courted by a young Sean Connery but married Ron. In the kindest sense, we all wondered why.

Ron was totally bonkers.

On one glittering occasion, Penny brought along Philip Lowrie, whom I knew from my days on *Coronation Street*. He played Dennis Tanner. Philip went upstairs to find the loo and, by mistake, entered the bird room. All hell broke loose — the birds went mad, shrieking and cawing at the interruption. Philip nearly had a heart attack!

Wendy rushed upstairs, into the raucous uproar, where she found the quivering Philip. "Stop! Stop it at once!" she commanded — and proceeded to sing. "This old man, he played one, he played knick-knack on my thumb — *Philip, it's next door on the right!* — With a knick-knack, paddy-whack, give a dog a bone…"

Philip staggered out as the birds started dancing on their perches. I had followed Wendy upstairs and looked upon a little African grey parrot muttering at the bottom of its cage.

"Who's this?"

"Timmy."

"What's he saying?"

"Lean in."

"Rat at the window, rat at the window," said Timmy.

"Why is he saying 'Rat at the window'?"

"Timmy can't say squirrel."

* * *

Still digressing, there was the occasion I met Yehudi Menuhin, the famed Austrian violinist and conductor. Paddy Foy, who had worked with him a lot, received a message. He wanted her to come to tea with Someone From BBC Children's Programmes.

I'd do.

"That's nice of Yehudi Menuhin to ask us to tea. I'm a great fan," I said as we drove in her car to Highgate.

"Hmmmm. Nice," she said, suspiciously.

Her suspicions were right.

Yehudi Menuhin received us and welcomed us into his drawing room, where the tea was prepared. Paddy introduced me: "Jeremy does *Jackanory* on children's television."

"Perfect," said Sir Yehudi and called out, "Diana, they're here!"

Lady Menuhin pirouetted into the room, showing us she still had the talent of a ballet dancer.

"My darling," declared the maestro. "It's your birthday and as a present from me, you will tell your children's stories on *Jackanory*! This is Jeremy. He's the director!"

Paddy and I were gobsmacked. Lady Menuhin radiated happiness at her adoring husband for his lovely birthday present. I gabbled small talk. Sir Yehudi beamed at the realisation of this sweet birthday present, bestowed upon his beloved wife.

In the car, on our departure, I said to Paddy, "Well, she can't. *Jackanory* is very selective. There are loads lined up — Eileen Atkins is to do *The Tailor of Gloucester* and Kenneth Williams is doing *Tales of Incrediblania* by Norman Hunter. Lady Menuhin's children's stories might be crap!"

Paddy was grim.

"Jeremy, this is dangerous. The last time there was any transgression of Menuhin's wishes it resulted in him banning all of his performances on the BBC. You'd better see Monica Sims when you get back. Our little tea party will put the wind up her."

It did. Monica was fully aware of the musical power Yehudi Menuhin exuded over the Corporation's classical output. Whatever Monica did, the Menuhin threat moved away. Paddy wiped her brow and had to contend with a Menuhin commemorative performance by the temperamental and brilliant Nigel Kennedy, who refused to turn up.

Monica said to me, "Well, that was a close shave."

Perhaps Lady Menuhin's Children's stories might have been wonderful. But we never found out. Maybe they were.

As for Monica Sims — well, I've already said how terrific she was. A BBC goddess. Even when she was heading BBC Radio 4, she remained unfailingly loyal to her old staff in Children's Programmes, along with Anna and me.

Monica lived in a big chaotic flat in Bayswater — always a great time there, and a lot of laughs. She moved to Richmond Villages, a retirement community in Painswick. Anna and I visited. "I started in a small room and now I'm finishing in a small room," mused Monica.

The small room afforded her a garden. I thought back to her garden in Bayswater, with a spiral staircase to a garage where stored her huge car.

Edward Barnes drove her home after a do one time. She went inside

IS THAT YOU, MAUREEN?

and Edward zoomed off through Bayswater. He paused in his car, to allow a lady to cross a zebra crossing. He started the engine and the lady hopped into his passenger seat.

"Hello, darling! Fancy a good time?"

She got out as Edward stammered, "How nice to meet you. Goodnight!" Home he went to Dorothy in Mortlake.

When Dorothy died there was a big funeral held at a church in Barnes. Every gem from each oratorio was sung. All quite beautiful, except for a nervous moment when the grandchildren decided to play "Housey!" under grandma's coffin. Paddy and I left the service. On the way out, I said, "Well, if that didn't get her up there, nothing will."

Paddy wanted the loo — so we nipped into a nearby pub. When we left, the entire funeral procession was passing, with accusatory eyes: "They've been on the piss!"

The wake was held in Second Avenue in Barnes, a stone's throw from the Thames. We toasted dear Dorothy with Anne and Tim Manderson, Edward's best friends. They became dear friends of mine, too.

Scene 10

Why do the wrong people travel?

Every year the Mandersons would rent a splendid villa in the south of France for a month and invite friends to stay. Careful casting informed every invitation issued by Tim and Annie. It wasn't always Saint-Tropez; one year was Majorca. I was a guest on a few occasions and they were idyllic days.

Tim was the most marvellous cook and he and Anne were wonderful hosts. "Today, it's poolside or light shopping," Tim would intone. Derek Deane was always there. He'd liven up any house party — not for nothing was he a genius choreographer.

After a while, Derek wanted to reciprocate so he rented a villa in Saint-

Tropez. I travelled out with him, driving the hire car. He'd been banned from driving that year due to some trivial prang in Chiswick. I was a very bad driver.

"Ditch, Jerry!" Derek kept shouting, as we approached La Jacaranda, our villa. Unfortunately, illness, other dates and prior engagements, made Derek and me the sole occupants of La Jacaranda. He took the west wing, me the east. We got on very well.

Moored in Saint-Tropez was Dodi Al Fayed's yacht, containing Dodi and his girlfriend, Diana — the Princess of Wales and a great friend of Derek's; she was a patron of the English National Ballet, where he was the Artistic Director.

A few days later, Derek yelled to me from the west wing, "Jerry! What's in the fridge by way of lunch?"

I got out of the pool and dripped into the kitchen to look in the fridge. "There's only some alien," I called back. 'Alien' was a local dish of octopus tentacles swimming in olive oil, looking like it had hopped out of John Hurt's stomach — hence the name.

"Not enough, Jerry! Nip to Spar. Princess of Wales is coming to lunch!"

Well, I nipped pretty smartly and loaded my trolley with every possible delicacy — bread, meats, salads — ready for a culinary frenzy back at the villa, fit for a nearly queen.

The phone rang.

"She's not coming, Jerry. She's off to Paris with Dodi."

Derek and I lived on the Princess' intended lunch for the rest of the holiday.

***

Keeping the vacation vein... Every summer, when we were children, Daddy would rent a house for us all to stay in. We went to Bray, Portrane and Achill Island.

In Portrane, our holiday house was next to a bigger one inhabited by a bigger family. They had ten children — one of whom, little Rosin, grew up to become Ros Hubbard, Ireland's most famous film casting director.

When we Swans stayed at the Matchbox on Achill Island, the family next door were the Fitzgeralds. Little Caroline Fitzgerald became a lifelong friend and a skilled theatrical director.

In the '60s I used to go to Ibiza before it became *Eye*-biza, where I'd stay with Eddy and Kathleen Lindsay-Hogg. Eddy had been married to the Irish film star Geraldine Fitzgerald before Kathleen; Geraldine was also the niece of Shelah, my landlady at Greenfield Manor.

Kathleen used to stay in Greenfield Manor while her husband stayed at the Stephen's Green Club, a private members' joint. They had a house in Ibiza too.

The Lindsay-Hogg house was on the coast, outside the town of San Antonio — perfect for a summer holiday but a nightmare in the winter. The Balearic Islands were notorious for their winters. I spent nearly all my time in the sea. Eddy and Kathleen eventually had a big house built in the middle of the Island. They invited me to stay.

Eddy was somewhat prone to hysteria when the drink got to him, prompting great rantings into the night. "Get me off this Devil's Island! I'm doomed!" he'd cry, adding — somewhat insensitively — "Why did I ever leave Geraldine? Why am I stuck in this forsaken place?"

Kathleen responded with a benign demeanour which I did my best to adopt too.

The morning after saw Eddy nursing a guilty demeanour.

"Jeremy, would you go to the neighbours and, er... tell them that we were, er... rehearsing a play last night and, er... hope it didn't disturb them."

The whole island had heard the rehearsal!

I walked to the next house, further up the road. It turned out that the neighbours were as benign about the theatrics as Kathleen. They were the Gibbs, whose sons were the Bee Gees. Like all the other expats in Ibiza, they were agog for any of the luscious gossip which abounded on the Island. A little house nearby was the love nest of Queen Soraya of Iran and French movie star Jean-Paul Belmondo. Kathleen confirmed this by standing on a dustbin and peering through a window one night while we were waiting for a bus to go into Ibiza town.

There was a club in the island's capital called La Tierra, where *everyone* went. The main source of gossip was Sandy Pratt — a delight who owned Sandy's Bar in Santa Eulària. What you didn't hear in the night in La Tierra you could hear the following day at Sandy's Bar.

The red-hot gossip at the time was about a fairly adequate artist who wasn't as fairly adequate as we thought — Elmyr de Hory, a Hungarian. He was a genius who had become one of the world's greatest forgers. Few galleries in the world can say with confidence whether the Modigliani on their wall is the real McCoy or one of Elmyr's knock-offs.

An American in Ibiza, Clifford Irving, wrote a book about Elmyr, titled *Fake*. Orson Welles made the movie *F is for Fake*, which he wrote, directed and starred in. Clifford Irving was not above his own skulduggery. He conned McGrath-Hill, the mighty publishing house, saying he had access to the notorious recluse Howard Hughes, and got a deal to write the famed movie director's autobiography. Hughes had invented a tantalising bra for Jane Russell, among other Hollywood highlights.

Irving was advanced a huge amount — enough for him to go on a 'research' trip to Nevada with his mistress Nina van Pallandt, one half of the singing duo Nina and Frederik. His wife, Edith, not knowing of the affair, dutifully lodged great dollops of dough at a bank in Zurich.

I saw Edith Irving at Ibiza airport. We were both on a plane to Zurich. She saw me. We politely averted our gazes — neither wanting to sit with a virtual stranger on a flight, one boring the pants off the other. I felt a bit guilty on arrival in Zurich. I saw her go into the Ladies so I waited, just to say hello. She never emerged. Well, she did. But bewigged with big sunglasses, on her way to the bank in disguise!

McGrath-Hill was still shovelling mountains of cash to Irving. What could possibly go wrong? The notoriously recluse Howard Hughes stopped being notoriously reclusive and blew the gaff to McGrath-Hill — that he didn't know Clifford Irving from Adam! Irving went to prison. So did his wife. Switzerland didn't like dealing with dodgy money. Dodgy Clifford then wrote another book in prison, *The Hoax* — cashing in on the whole Hughes con. His shenanigans continued to enthral. It's a good book, as good as *Fake* — read it!

***

At the Lindsay-Hogg house in Ibiza, we were joined by Lucy Davies. She had been momentarily married to Eddy Lindsay-Hogg's son, Michael. We'd all been lodgers back at Greenfield Manor in Dublin — Michael, Lucy and I, all working for RTÉ.

Lucy was a joy and much loved by her ex-in-laws. Back in London, she became a PA at the BBC, having been a PA at RTÉ. She lived near me, in Kensington Square; I was in Vicarage Gate, up the road. She later married

Tony Snowdon, the ex of Princess Margaret — and thus became the Countess of Snowdon. When Lucy left Kensington, she gave me all her furniture — among the pieces, the chair in which I am sitting writing this. Eddy's son Michael became a famous director of theatre, TV and music videos — working with the Rolling Stones and the Beatles. He's now a famous painter. In the theatre, when Michael used to do his smouldering Orson Welles impression, we would call him 'Sparkler'. The real Orson never sparkled! Michael and I were at the Gaiety when Orson Welles was appearing in *Chimes at Midnight*, directed by Hilton Edwards. We called the great man 'Orson Cart' behind his back.

Michael was Hilton's assistant, while I was a passing ASM. *Chimes at Midnight* was a brilliant play by Orson — pulling all the Fullstaff scenes from the Shakespearean Henrys to make a *big* part in which he shone.

Tho' he was nearly outshone by Keith Baxter playing Henry V.

* * *

A few years prior to my Ibiza introduction, Shelah Richards told myself and Wendy Shea, artist and RTÉ designer, that we should go to Nerja in Spain for a holiday. "It's very easy to get there. When you arrive in Malaga, turn left."

Wendy and I decided to get there by an adventurous route. We flew to Cherbourg and took a train to Paris. We stayed a night in the Hotel du Mont Blanc off Place Saint-Michel — one of my old haunts of the *Saint Joan* tour. From Paris, it was a train to Hendaya on the Spanish border — and thence a train to Malaga, down through Central Spain.

It took two days. We sat on creaky wooden seats and grabbed bocadillos from the women who sold them at station platforms along the route. The landscape changed visibly on our rickety train journey — from fertile to arid, getting ever hotter.

Eventually, we reached Malaga and hopped on a bus going to Nerja. We got rooms in a small hotel owned by the mistress of the local priest. The only other tenants were an old Englishman, Colonel Marsh, and his servant, Incana. Nerja was very quaint. In the evenings, everyone would sit at tables and drink the local plonk. During the day, we would go to the beach at the Balcón de Europa hotel and walk along the lower slopes of the Sierra Nevada. It was all very idyllic.

All sorts observed on the Costa del Sol

I decided to go to Tangiers, where a friend from RTÉ was in residence. Wendy wanted no more travelling, so I got the bus from Nerja to Gibraltar alone — teetering along an awful highway that formed a tarmac sliver between land and sea.

I was only slightly aware of the political rumblings going on at La Linea. I tried to get a ferry at Gibraltar but there was no ferry. So I had to get another bus to Algeciras to catch a boat there. Franco had been stirring things up at the Gib. All these trips required me to cash travellers' cheques from the Bank of Ireland. "You're lucky you're not with the Bank of England," the Banco de España cashier mused darkly — another hint of Franco's creepy intents against *extranjeros* in Spain and resentment over the British ownership of Gibraltar. The boat trip from Algeciras to Tangiers was marred. I dropped my expensive Yashica overboard while photographing a flying fish.

I spent a day in Tangiers. It's probably changed its act since then, but at the time, it had a sordid and raffish air. That probably accounted for my friend Brian from RTÉ for being there. He was sordid and raffish. Joe Orton and Kenneth Halliwell used to go there on their holidays — they were sordid and raffish too.

The air was pungent with hashish and incense. Squinting at the address, I found Brian's lodgings. There was a forbidding notice nailed to the closed door, pronouncing that the establishment had been closed by the police and that all enquiries should be referred to the local gaol! The notice was written in authoritative French.

I swiftly abandoned the search for my friend. God only knew where he was and I wasn't going to look. I decided to head back to Wendy in Nerja. I took a wander through the bazaars and souks; then to a post office to send a card to the parents. I strolled into the labyrinth of the Casbah. I looked into a bar, contemplating a drink. At the end of a long, dark counter, two Americans were knocking it back.

"Come in!" yelled the man.

"Join us, do!" cried his female companion.

Introductions were made — they were Tennessee Williams and Barbara Hutton, the Woolworths heiress. They were pleasantly plastered. He was researching a play, she was spending the money. They were drinking strange, cloudy, green drinks from a jug that had a herby bouquet sticking out of the top.

"Tom has a major talent," Miss Hutton slurred.

I knew. I said I loved his *A Streetcar Named Desire.*

"There are a lot of Blanche DuBoises in this town!" he exclaimed. "Hang on in, the rest will be here soon! Have another drink, Jeremy!"

I thought it wise not to; with pleasant goodbyes and kisses, I sidled off. This would be an encounter to tell Wendy — if I ever got back to Nerja!

I found the ferry point for Gibraltar and sat in the cafeteria. No sign of that pleasant herby drink I'd had with Tennessee Williams and Barbara Hutton. I think I was a bit woozy. I was joined by another American.

"I'm Alex Quackenbush." Americans always tell you who they are. The surname was early Pennsylvanian, he explained. Americans always explain. "Can you do me a favour, Jeremy? I'm in the American Legation in Malaga."

Oh, cripes!

"Can you take a bicycle on the ferry?"

"Why can't you take your own bicycle on the ferry?"

"There's two. I've got the other one. I can't manage two."

Fair enough. We got the two bicycles from the bike park and trundled them to the ferry. One of the bikes was for his friend, who also worked for the American Legation in Malaga.

At Gibraltar, there was major consternation. People getting on and off. Passport chaos. No exit until the next day. Alex Quackenbush got a room in the British Royal Overseas Hostel for us — plus the bikes. Wendy must have thought that I was dead! Or murdered by the missing Brian, of whom she was rightly suspicious.

The next day, we pushed the bikes across Gibraltar to La Linea — the Spanish border. Mr Quackenbush had all the necessary diplomatic passes. Onto a bus, the bikes on the roof. There were a lot of militaries at La Linea. My Irish passport was scrutinised. At Malaga, we unloaded the bicycles. Mr Quackenbush's colleague was waiting to collect his. So, we said farewell. Alex Quackenbush gave me his card.

Another bus to Nerja.

Wendy was very unwell when I finally reached her. I suspected some concoction stewed up by the mistress of the priest. She had been looked after by Colonel Marsh and Incana.

"We've got to get back to Ireland," I told her. "You're sick!"

We then discovered that all the trains from Malaga were up the spout, due to the international situation. We were marooned!

But no — we weren't! I phoned Alex Quackenbush. He arranged for us to get a diplomatic train from Malaga to Madrid. Not only that, but he also fixed it so we could stay in a US flat in the Atocha district of the Spanish capital. The man was a saint!

We found the flat — a great flat too! — keys were exchanged, and we were left with a night to figure out how to get from Madrid to Paris. We made it to Paris, though was Wendy still very ill — and the interminable train journey did not speed her recovery. At the Hotel du Mont Blanc in Paris we had to get a doctor, who fixed her up. After a train to Cherbourg and a plane, our respective parents welcomed us back to Dublin. Wendy was whisked to her parents' home in Sandymount, Dad drove me back to Shelah at Greenfield Manor.

"Did you both have a lovely time?" she asked.

"Yes, terrific."

*People waiting for a bus in Valladolid, Mexico.
The ladies on the left obviously had assignations*

A Christmas card design for the Actors' Benevolent Fund

Scene 11

Crime and punishment

Where was I? I'd better get a bit chronological. So, back at the BBC. I was still busy producing *Rentaghost* and *Grandad* starring Clive Dunn — both shows written by Bob Block.

Clive Dunn was a genius to work with. We depicted Grandad as a mischievous old git. The main joy of the rehearsals was Clive's great stories. He told me about a celebrity lunch at Downing Street, hosted by the Prime Minister, Harold Wilson, to honour the cast of *Dad's Army*.

Mr Wilson extolled the glory of the cast: "A band of men whose talents have delighted the British public for decades. A band of actors whose sole vocation was to entertain and delight the British public. Actors have a God-given talent that they share with their delighted audiences. Actors are—"

John Laurie interrupted the Prime Minister's eulogy, with his broad Scottish accent. "Ye forgot one thing, Prime Minister."

"And what's that, Mr Laurie?"

"Ye forgot to say that all actors are cunts!"

Another tale of Clive's. He'd been touring with a play which wasn't doing very well. In some provincial theatre, ten minutes before curtain up, the stage manager peeped through the tabs. "It's a disaster out there! There's only one big fat chap sitting in the middle of the stalls!"

"Never mind," declared Clive. "The cast and I will line up on stage. You'll bring up the curtain and I'll tell the loyal theatrical soul that we'll do the entire play just for him."

The curtain went up. Clive and the cast stood there.

"Thank you for being here, my friend," Clive announced. "There may be only one of you out there tonight but, as dedicated actors, we will perform the entire play, just for you, from start to finish."

"Well, get a move on," the man shouted from the stalls. "I'm waiting to lock up!"

Clive had a wonderful ear for nuance and for finding the laughs. One day, he seized upon a script typo — the 't' had been left out of the word 'stock'. At the read-through, Clive read, "If word gets out about this, Mr Watkins, I'll be a laughing sock!"

We recorded the *Grandad* shows in a great new BBC complex on Oxford Road in Manchester — which replaced the original BBC Studios housed in a converted church on Dickenson Road. After the first series, Clive

CRIME AND PUNISHMENT

insisted that we bring in an audience of kids for the recordings and he turned out to be dead right. They loved us — and they really laughed.

On the first recording day, the gram operator, a classical music fan, played some Requiem music as the audience filed in; lilting sounds of Mozart filled the studio. The time came for Clive to come out and do the warm-up. He listened the melody and asked, "Has the Director-General died?"

We switched to more jovial music after that.

Early on, Clive Dunn's character had a pet macaw parrot, organised by Wendy Duggan. On the recording, Clive came in and said to the parrot, "Good morning." The parrot, instead of replying "Good morning", came down from its perch, positioned itself in the camera sights, and did a little dance, to everyone's delight.

The bird had a taste of fame now and there was no stopping it. Soon, no scene passed without it suddenly flapping its wings or some other ruthless attempt at upstaging.

Clive made an ultimatum: "Either the parrot goes, or I go."

"Actually, Clive, the parrot is quite good."

* * *

Doing *Grandad* in Manchester was part of an overall BBC strategy. The regional studios wanted a taste of network transmissions, but the trouble was they didn't have enough expertise. I had been sent to direct *Potter's Picture Palace*, starring Melvyn Hayes, Angela Crow, John Comer, Colin Edwynn and Eden Phillips. It was set in an old cinema. They had already done with one series when I arrived. For the second run, I became the BBC TV Centre hatchet man. I thought this was all very unfair — the previous episodes had been directed very well. But BBC London dictated it so. The producer, John Buttery, welcomed me warmly, as if I were the greatest director since Zeffirelli!

I'd also done an earlier show at BBC Manchester — *Plum's Plots and Plans*, starring Arthur Howard as an eccentric inventor and explorer. The cast included Aubrey Woods and William Hootkins, who went on to appear in *Star Wars*. One script necessitated a cooker blowing up.

"We'll do a test during the lunch break," Peter Pegrum, the visual effects director, told me. During lunch in the canteen, while having my grub with the cast, the entire building shuddered with a huge explosion.

"Christ almighty! Was that a bomb?"
No. Just Peter Pegram doing his test.

* * *

We rehearsed *Grandad* in London — so going up to Manchester was a major hassle. My BBC office used to turn into a travel agency: trains had to be arranged, along with digs and taxis the day before the shooting in Manchester. We'd meet on a train at Euston — all the actors going dotty, leaving girlfriends and wives to go and work up North.

We stayed in digs in Levenshulme at Harry and Marjorie Hoey's house Harry was the Scenic Operational Manager at the BBC studios. His wife, Marjorie, was our landlady. "Be very quiet when you go upstairs," she warned. "Lila Kaye, the actress, is sleeping next to the bathroom. Jeremy, you're in your usual room. Clive is in Audrey's, next door."

We'd made a detour to a pub between Manchester Piccadilly Station and Levenshulme to recover from the train journey from London. I think there had been a bit of recovery on the train as well. A lot of *sssshhhes* and stumbles were heard as we headed to the rooms, followed by flushing and the sounds of rigorous toothbrushing from the one bathroom.

The next morning, there were early departures for the actors, due in costume and make-up. I required neither, so would follow on to start camera rehearsals at 10am. As I came out of my room, my way was blocked by a large dressing-gowned woman clutching the bannister rail.

"Don't speak! Don't speak! Thirty-two people went to the lavatory last night! I was trying to sleep next door!"

This was Lila Kaye, the actress. Later, she came into the kitchen as I was finishing my breakfast. Marjorie introduced us. Miss Kaye had calmed down and was dressed to face the day.

"Lila is in *Crime and Punishment* at the Royal Exchange," Marjorie announced. "I'm longing to see it so I've got tickets for tomorrow night, Jeremy. Nothing like a bit of Dostoyevsky! You'll be finished editing. Harry can't come. He'll be still getting your set out of the studio."

We usually shot the show on Thursday, edited it on Friday and on Saturday headed back to London.

Lila was delighted by the news. "Be sure to book the restaurant for after, Marjorie. It's Russian-themed. You can never go wrong with a plate of plov!"

CRIME AND PUNISHMENT

"Who are you playing?" I asked.

"I'm the *Crime* — I'm over in half an hour. The *Punishment* goes on for three hours after that!"

My taxi came. I went to the BBC studios in Oxford Road and recorded the show. The actors went back on late trains to London. We'd then all meet again in the North Acton rehearsal rooms on Monday to rehearse the next episode.

The next night, Marjorie and I were in the front row of the Royal Exchange Theatre for *Crime and Punishment*, directed by Braham Murray. Lila was the Pawnbroker — not a bird-like woman, as described by Dostoyevsky, but a large, glittering, evil one with a big beehive wig and a black jet dress. Clever Braham Murray! Raskolnikov, played by Tom Courtney, duly bashed Lila to death — and the Pawnbroker's sister — with a candlestick. The set swivelled and transformed to the misty streets of St Petersburg, with Tom Courtney staggering upstage, ominously followed by the figure of the Detective Inspector, Leo McKern. Marjorie and I were watching enthralled. Suddenly, our knees were gripped by unseen hands. It was the Crime, crawling offstage.

She whispered, "Have you booked the restaurant, Marjorie?"

Marjorie nodded assent, somewhat startled.

"Good! It's my treat — I get ten percent off!" said Lila, as she scuttled into the darkness.

Lila became a darling friend and a brilliant acquisition in many shows that I produced later on. One of which was a pantomime. Annual pantos fell under my producer brief at BBC's Children's Programmes. Among them was Lila Kaye's panto. I dashed off a script with Jim Eldridge — *Jack and the Beanstalk*.

A snag, but a delightful one — the Chuckle Brothers were to star. So it became *Jacks and the Beanstalk*. "Mother only liked two names — Jack and Daisy. She called the cow Daisy, and she called us Jack!"

Lila was mother.

"What was Daddy like?" asked the Jacks.

"I'll tell you," said Lila, launching with gusto into *Boogie Woogie Bugle Boy* by Company B. Hardly camp at all!

I did another pantomime, a biggie, *Aladdin and the Forty Thieves*. We had to call it that — there were so many people who wanted to be in it. I engaged John Morley, a famed pantomime writer, through my agent,

IS THAT YOU, MAUREEN?

Myrette Morven. I'd inherited her from Paul Ciani, the original *Rentaghost* producer. Myrette was one of the founders of Fraser and Dunlop, a big London agency.

Sarah Greene, a refugee from *Blue Peter*, was to play Aladdin. Jan Francis, then a big BBC star, was the Princess. Johnny Morris was the Widow Twanky, Terry Nutkins was Wishee Washee and *Grange Hill*'s Todd Carty was Ali Baba. Kenneth Connor played the chief of the forty thieves, with Brian Cant as the Emperor of China, Ann Emery as the Empress, Clive Dunn as the Grand Vizier and Kenneth Williams as a storyteller. Christopher Biggins and Floella Benjamin were the genies of the lamp and the ring, and Eddy Brayshaw was Abanazar. The rest of the cast included Molly Weir, Hal Dyer and a lot of BBC Children's celebs. John Asquith and Bill Perrie were Ali Baba's horse Dobbin, borrowed from *Rentaghost*. Plus we had newsreaders John Craven, Barry Took and pretty much anyone else who was hanging around the BBC. There was a huge set, comprising the Imperial Palace of Peking, caves, market squares and laundries, even a side trip to Egypt — all constructed in Television Centre's biggest studio, TC1.

In no way would a show like this be performed in today's climate of sensitivity. From Floella Benjamin's declaring, "*Cha* man! What do you mean black magic?" during the Genie of the Ring's first appearance, to Christopher Biggins announcing as he emerged from his lamp, "Thank goodness, I thought no one would ever rub it," we offended all and sundry down the line.

Kenneth Williams, playing Mustafa Drink, got to yell at the muezzin's prayer to the faithful, "Shut yer row up!" He then launched into a funny story, delivered to camera, concerning three telephoning Emperors. The punchline: "Whenever the Emperor rang Wing, he got a Wong number!"

Well. That sort of script would be enough to launch a missile strike these days.

Later, I handled the pantomimes for *Blue Peter*, including *A Christmas Carol*, butchered from Charles Dickens. Anthea Turner was Scrooge, Diane-Louise Jordan played the Christmas Spirits and six-foot-three John Leslie was Tiny Tim. It was *avant-garde*!

One year, theatrical producer Lee Dean asked me to direct *Jack and the Beanstalk* at the Lyceum in Crewe, starring Mark Curry as Jack and Carmen Silvera as the Fairy Queen. The stage management was a bit dodgy. On the first night at the end of Act I, a stagehand noticed that the beanstalk was not properly tied off in the flies.

As Mark heroically mounted the beanstalk, there was a yell from the wings. "Don't climb that beanstalk!"

The curtain hastily came down.

All these exhaustive thoughts of pantomimes make me want to get back on course...

Scene 12
Going south

Edward Barnes had been appointed the new BBC Head of Children's Programmes; Anna Home was the Head of Children's Drama. I was busy with *Rentaghost*. Michael Staniforth played Timothy Claypole, a medieval jester-poltergeist. We were forced to get rid of the appellation 'poltergeist' because the film *The Exorcist* had recently come out, so he became a sprite — a renaming suitably distanced from any connotations of 360-degree head-swivelling or uttering of guttural obscenities.

Michael was hugely talented. He sang the signature tune — *Rentaghost*'s, not *The Exorcist*'s. And he became a big star in West End musicals — *A Chorus Line*, *Sweeney Todd* and later *Starlight Express*, where he displayed his roller-skating skills. His stage appearances meant all his *Rentaghost* scenes had to be shot before 6pm. We always made sure that afternoon matinees didn't coincide with the recording days. Heavies from the West End would appear in the studio to whisk him off to the theatre.

Michael was sadly swooped up by the dreaded spectre of AIDS which took so many at the time.

Then came a severe jolt. Anna was leaving the BBC to set up TVS, a new TV company in the south of England. Edward was hopping mad! He hopped higher when she invited me to join her. I accepted her invitation and produced the ninth and final series of *Rentaghost* before leaving the BBC for TVS.

I was living in my house in Battersea. This new job necessitated that I live in Maidstone. Pondering this, I went on a holiday to stay with Clive Dunn and his wife, Priscilla Morgan, in the Algarve in Portugal. Clive was doing a stand-up in a local hotel and one of the dancers, Wendy, came up with the solution to my Maidstone problem. She knew people who had an oast house for rent in Willington, near Maidstone. The oast house had been retired from hop brewing but still had the little pointed turrets. It was quaint and perfect! Meanwhile, my friends Eddy and Kathleen Lindsay-Hogg were looking for a place to stay while on their annual escape from Ibiza. They could have my house.

I asked my neighbours, Diana Smith and Ken Sharp, who had houses opposite, to keep an eye on them. Diana had a low tolerance level and the Lindsay-Hoggs were intolerant so it was not the happiest of surveillances. Ken got on with them OK. He was a senior designer at the BBC, working, around that time with Paddy Foy on *The Magic of the Dance* with Margot Fonteyn. The Lindsay-Hoggs loved this connection with all the grandeur of the Ballet world.

As a director at TVS, I was given *Fraggle Rock*, a brilliant programme produced by the magical Jim Henson Organisation. I liked puppets. They never answered back but, by jingo, the puppeteers did! *Fraggle Rock* was fronted by Fulton McKay — a star of *Porridge* — and a puppet dog called Sprocket. To say I directed *Fraggle Rock* doesn't ring true. All the nitty-gritty of the show was filmed in Canada. All I had to do was knit the links with Fulton and the dog. The grit had already been done.

The producer was Duncan Kenworthy and the scriptwriter was Victor Pemberton. Fulton was temperamental. So was Victor. Duncan was the referee. My PA Pam Brown and I silently surveyed script wars. I liked Fulton. I liked temperament. I must have — when I think of my long cast list! All Fulton had to do was to present the show with a puppet dog. It wasn't exactly *King Lear*!

The series was shot in Gillingham, a stubborn Medway town, in an old cinema that had been converted into a TV studio. It was also the venue for my next assignment, directing *Afternoon Club*. This was a magazine programme that TVS envisaged as a force to showcase Kent's Medway towns. That didn't work. We quickly bussed in the audience from posher Tunbridge Wells.

Afternoon Club was presented by Una Stubbs, David 'Kid' Jensen and Lucy Morgan. For one gripping item, we brought in a psychotherapist, Phillip Hodson, to interview people with mental hangups. Among them, there was a compulsive shoplifter, who insisted on being interviewed in impenetrable silhouette because of her notoriety. The floor manager led her to a chair before the questioning shrink. The woman waffled on about how she started shoplifting — first sweets, then household goods. She was in her stride but my colleagues in the control room were dozing off. Then I noticed — with horror — that the lights were beginning to creep up, revealing the shoplifter in her notorious glory! She was in full flow about stealing furniture when I heard police sirens. The local cop shop had been watching *Afternoon Club*.

Our next victim for televisual psychotherapeutic interrogation was a woman who was set off by any colloquial stress. She was put into the chair as the shoplifter was ushered to the studio doors. There was a phalanx of police waiting for her. "Gotcha!"

Phillip gently asked his next guest, "What triggers your problem?"

"Shouting, obscenities."

At the door, the shoplifter yelled, "You *bastards*! You set me up! You *shits*!"

The vocal-stressed woman had the abdabs.

We used to put plants in the audience with questions to pep up the interviewers when things on air began getting limp — actors Helen Cottrell and Anthony Smee. One afternoon, Una Stubbs was interviewing a worthy woman who excelled in macramé, the art of knitting string. It was not going well.

"And when did you go on to hanging baskets?" yawned Una.

"I started with yoghurt pots."

Time for a directorial intervention. "Go to the plant!" I hissed into Una's earpiece. The set consisted of sofas for the audience, sprinkled with greenery planted in jardinières. It looked like a furniture showroom. Una glazed at my command, obviously not understanding to ask the actors for a primed research question. "Go to the plant!" I bellowed.

The interviewee was still rabbiting on. "String is so important. I use a woven coir..."

Una suddenly stood up and started to glide away from the interview base.

"Where the hell is she going? Cameras! Stay with her! Stay with her!"

Una stopped gliding and stood beside a wilting banana tree.

"I'm with the plant... erm... whose leaves are shredded into strips... erm... for macramé twine..."

The phone rang in the control room. It was Anna, Controller of TVS.

"What the *hell* is going on down there?"

* * *

TVS then sent me to direct *Farmers' Report*, but there's only so much about silage that can grab you. And then it was *Coast to Coast*, a news magazine programme. I had to go to the TVS Southampton studios to direct that. I drove down in my Mini. John Jones, the station manager, warned me that I'd have to stay overnight in the Polygon Hotel in Southampton after transmission due to directorial exhaustion. The Polygon was known as the Dead Parrot. The bore was that *Coast to Coast* was on the air from 6.30 till 7.00pm. I was doomed to twelve hours in the Polygon. After the show, I was wandering aimlessly through the empty corridors of the Southampton studios when I heard the pop of a wine bottle opening. In an office was Anna and a lively lady.

"Who are you?" she asked, as I timorously entered.

"I'm Jeremy. I'm the director of *Coast to Coast*."

"He is," said Anna.

"Of course he is! Come in. Have a drink!"

And that's how I met Theresa Plummer-Andrews, who we called 'Trees'. She was Head of Programme Acquisition at TVS.

"I'm staying up here in the Polygon," I explained. "I'm worried about getting back to the oast house in Maidstone. Horace is on his own."

"Who's Horace? The boyfriend?"

"No, the parrot."

Horace was a cockatiel that Wendy Duggan had given me. I traipsed him around in a very expensive Harrod's cage. When I turned up at TVS, my staff thought I was Long John Silver.

Trees turned out to be the greatest gas — I'd met a new friend.

TVS was getting a bit uncomfortable. I think *Farmers' Report* clinched it for me. Meanwhile, back in Battersea, the Lindsay-Hoggs were wreaking havoc in my house. When I occasionally went back, I recoiled. Diana

Smith had cooked a meal which nearly killed them.

I fled back to the oast house and rang my ex-BBC PA, Jillie Sutton, for a chat. "How's it going?" she asked.

"Well. Not so good. Horace the parrot has got a cold. The oast house is bloody freezing. Storage heaters don't work! And I'm not getting any good shows at TVS."

"Ring Edward," she suggested. "He's always asking how you are. Give him a buzz."

"He won't want to hear from me, having defected!"

"He'll love to hear from you," Jillie insisted.

So I rang Edward. Dorothy, his wife answered.

"Ed... Ed, it's Jeremy!"

Edward's voice came on the line. "How are you, darling?"

"Well, Edward. This job is a bit duff."

"Goodbye!"

He hung up.

Oh. Not the best phone call!

Early next morning, my phone rang in the oast house.

"Hello. Jeremy, this is George Ageros."

I knew George — he was the manager of Children's Programmes. He was at his most pompous. "I've been instructed to call you."

"Hi, George!"

"I've spoken to HCP." That meant Head of Children's Programmes — Edward. "He indicated that you might consider returning to us?"

Cue a rapid professional assessment.

"I'm on the pensionable staff here at TVS, thanks. So I'd only consider a similar post at the BBC."

In my office at TVS, I told Pam Brown, my loyal PA, of my machinations.

"Good for you! Get out of this joint. Greg Dyke has taken over."

The phone rang. It was BBC Personnel.

"We'd like to offer you a six-month contract as director in Children's Programmes at the BBC."

A contract? No way! Where's the permanent job? "I've got a pensionable job from ITV!" For TVS was part of that. "I'm not interested!"

A few moments later, the phone rang again.

"Hi, Jeremy. It's Edward. Have you heard from Personnel?"

"Yes, I did. I'm afraid it's not on, Edward. Much as I'd like to get back—"

"Goodbye!"

Click. He was gone. Well, that was that.

No, it wasn't! The phone rang — BBC Personnel again: "Sorry, we made a mistake." Good old Edward had intervened. "We'd like to offer you a permanent job, with full pension benefits, in BBC Children's Programmes!"

Jubillante! The next nightmare was to present Anna with my decision. She wasn't best pleased. She said I'd better go and talk to Greg Dyke. The little big man had his feet on the desk when I sat down before him in his office. That cemented my intention.

Anna asked me to accompany her to the TVS Christmas ball at a local hotel. I felt like Scarlett O'Hara turning up at Melanie's party but was sorry to say goodbye to the best of friends. Nigel Pickard held a dinner for me. He was Head of Children's Programmes at TVS and eventually became Head of Children's Programmes at the BBC.

Back at the Beeb, I arrived in the media mist of the New Year — everyone was on holiday. Best to rejoin in a certain amount of obscurity, I thought.

I was given my old office in the East Tower.

"We can't believe you are back!" said my colleagues, repeating their exclamation from when I returned from RTÉ. Neither could I.

The first job that Edward assigned to me was to direct *Albert, Prince of Treasure Houses* — an instalment of the documentary series *Treasure Houses*. His wife Dorothy wrote the script. Mark Curry was the presenter. We filmed at various sites and situs inspired or once inhabited by Queen Victoria's Consort. From the top of Knightsbridge Barracks, the camera could see the outline of the Crystal Palace in the grass of Hyde Park, where it was constructed for the Great Exhibition of the Works of Industry of all Nations in 1851. I had the camera pan left across the roofs of London, showing where it was later moved to and where it burned down. The south-west London suburb was named after Albert's transplanted building.

Filming at the Albert Memorial was threatened by Kensington Council deciding to close it down for restoration work on the days we were to film.

The Council was contrite. "Can you reschedule? It will only be closed for a day or two."

Luckily, we couldn't. So, they gave us an extra day.

The Albert Memorial was closed for nine years thereafter.

There are often hiccups that occur with filming that make you tear your hair out. One such hiccup occurred in the script. In front of the Memorial, Mark narrated, "So deep was the grief of the sorrowing Queen at the death of her beloved Albert that she commanded the finest erection in London to be built in his memory. And to this day, that erection is known as the Albert Memorial."

Cut! The crew were sniggering.

But the perfect professionalism of Mark Curry didn't display a titter.

I rang Edward Barnes, the producer of the series. "I want to change a word in the script, Edward. It doesn't sit comfortably."

"Don't change a word! Dorothy's script is perfect. What word do you want to change?"

"Erection."

"Ah. Change it to what?"

"Er... monument?" I was inspired!

Edward was so pleased with the finished programme that he gave me another *Treasure House* to direct: *Westminster Abbey* — the Coronation seat of Kings, steeped in history. For the opening shot, I put a camera on the front of a Number 11 bus going down Victoria Street. My assistant Robert Checksfield successfully negotiated with Scotland Yard to turn all of Victoria Street's traffic lights to green so that the Number 11 bus could drive by unhindered. I sat in the Methuselah wine bar with the rest of the crew as the bus went up and down Victoria Street. We dubbed Handel's *Zadok the Priest* over the progression.

A great thing came out of filming *Westminster Abbey*. It's how I met Stuart Holmes. He was the Head of Protocol at the Abbey and he's been my constant companion for over 30 years. Edward took great pride in augmenting the introduction. It was cemented by me asking Stuart along to see Ken Dodd at the Palladium. Wonderful Ken Dodd — "Boots, boots, marching over Africa!" with an avalanche of boots crashing from above.

Pursuing the date after the show, we went to Joe Allen's in Covent Garden for dinner. Oh dear... it wasn't the best table. My then-agent, Paul Spyker, came over and asked, "Why are you sitting at this shit table?"

The reason was that my unruly director friend Michael Kerrigan had booked a table the night before in my name, inviting Anna Home and Andrew Morgan to dine with him. Michael was soon crazy with the champagne. Anna and Andrew sloped off in terror as Michael ordered more bubbly.

IS THAT YOU, MAUREEN?

The restaurant was closing. The staff were having their supper at the bar. Behind them was the restaurant, where clattering and banging was heard. Michael was barricading the restaurant with chairs and tables!

"In whose name was the table booked for that lunatic?" demanded Richard Polo, the manager.

"Jeremy Swan. He's here tomorrow night with Stuart Holmes from Westminster Abbey."

"Give them a lousy table!"

They did. But the wonderful Stuart didn't seem to mind. After our date, I drove him to his flat in St George's Drive, Pimlico. There was no going in, but I asked him to dinner at my house a week later.

My closest friends Caroline Dawson and Neil Hardie wanted to meet Stuart. They did — and they loved him as much as I did. As did our respective parents. His mother, Joyce, said to me, "We are delighted that Stuart has got someone like you in his life at last."

My parents Una and Jack agreed. "Stuart is good news!"

He was — and is!

That's enough down the sloppy road.

Stuart in full pomp as Master of the Gold and Silver Wyre Drawers Livery

Above: The Boy Who Would be King. *I won Feis Ceoil 1953, Dublin.*
Right: My parents dressing down

A signed picture from
Micheál Mac Liammóir

Below: With John Gilmartin playing Hardcastle in She Stoops to Conquer *at St Mary's College I was an understated Kate*

With David Jordan, my school pal, in the school production of Charley's Aunt. *I played Jack Chesney*

SUNDAY INDEPENDENT, AUG. 7, 1966. PAGE 7. D

T.E. MAN LEAVING FOR LONDON

★ Pictured at a farewell party given in his honour at "Greenfields," Milltown Road, is Jeremy Swan, with Caroline Fitzgerald. Mr. Swan, who is a Floor Manager with Telefís Éireann and a well known theatre personality, will leave Dublin shortly for Granada Television, London.

Right: Rock Hudson snapped on the Captain Lightfoot *set by my hopelessly smitten aunt. Below: Shoving my face in the birthday cake at the celebration for* The School Around the Corner *at RTÉ, 1963*

With Anna McGoldrick for RTÉ's A Handful of Songs, 1970

1969, deep in thought

Happy days on Jackanory. *With Ann Beach, who read* Green Smoke

Kenneth Williams, in his contentious kaftan for The Land of Green Ginger

Above: Maurice Denham reading The Wind on the Moon.
Right: A bewigged Thora Hird for Mrs Pepperpot's Outing

Rehearsing The Hartwarp Light Railway *with George Layton*

Tom Merrifield, object of desire, in Jackanory's The Emperor's New Clothes

Directing on location in Manchester for Potter's Picture Palace

On location with the Rentaghost *boys — Michael Darbyshire, Anthony Jackson and Michael Staniforth*

Lynda Marchal — soon to emerge as Lynda La Plante — as the nanny ghost Tamara Novek

Rosemary Watson and Jillian Somers off Ascoting.
Right: Painting in Turkey

Below: Pensive in Venice

Above: Sara Randall,
my faithful agent
of many years.
Left: Vanya Kewley

With my friend
Caroline Dawson on
a night out in Venice

LOVE FROM Rentaghost!

The 1980s Rentaghost *cast: Molly Weir, Jeffrey Segal, Sue Nicholls, William Perrie and John Asquith inside Dobbin, Michael Staniforth, Edward Brayshaw, Hal Dyer and Ann Emery. Eddy Brayshaw drew the ghost logo*

Biggins and I, au jardin in Hackney. I had just unveiled his garden shed

Above: Schmoozing the Duchess of Kent, making a BBC visit in 1983. My explanation of Rentaghost *clearly thrilled her*

Above: Lila Kaye and Zulema Dene in Bad Boyes, *one of several shows I directed written by Jim Eldridge. Right: Shots from* Grandad, *kept by Clive Dunn*

Nigel Cooke with Robbie Swales, Kenneth Williams and Paul Wilce on Galloping Galaxies! *with Junior the robot— "Deddy, deddy!" Kenneth made him rather posh*

COURTESY OF GRAHAM KIBBLE-WHITE

*A party for
Uncle Jack
and Cleopatra's
Mummy in 1993.
Continuing my
love affair with
Fenella Fielding*

*A costume sketch for
Uncle Jack's colleague Dorothy,
as played by Tricia George*

*Fenella about to cut
a sarcophagus cake.
She made us rather
nervous with that knife*

With the monsters of Monster TV in 1999. I designed the costumes, worn by James O'Donnell, Anna Nicholas and John Asquith. Socks model's own

Directing A House That's Just Like Yours *in the gallery at Teddington Studios*

Setting up a shot with raised sets and monitors on the studio floor

In cramped quarters. There's no easy way to direct puppets

In Barbados for The Mikado, *directed by Christopher Biggins. My ship sailed better in the dark*

Sunning it with Brad Fitt, who would become a lasting friend

A card for Dame Biggins

The Mikado —
Barbados 1996

A LITTLE MAID FROM SCHOOL.

Rosie Ashe –
Liz Robertson –
Cory Pulman –

Japanese type pins.

a beret –

Black cloche wig –

Leg of mutton sleeves on shirt with collar – white chiffon – an over tunic with ribbons – mauve –

a girdle – black –

A gingham skirt – (courtesy of Jeannie Landry)

Hens bum knickers –

Black stockings, sheer.

Black or white plimsols

Jeremy '96

Above: Enjoying local life.
Left: A little maid design

Off the beaten track

OFF THE BEATEN TRACK Barbados

Local faces in Clapham Junction, my neighbourhood

Above: BBC colleagues Edward Barnes and Biddy Baxter at my art exhibition, held at the Omnibus

My back garden in Battersea, painted in full bloom

Dinner at Joe Allen's with Stuart Holmes, Theresa 'Trees' Plummer-Andrews and Anna Home

Above: With Stuart Holmes MVO, Member of the Victorian Order, in the gardens of Westminster Abbey

Van Goghing a Van Gogh on a recent gallery visit in London

A theatre trip with Brad Fitt, dressed in coincidental coats

Scene 13

Some people ♪

I'm going to digress again. You've already heard about Micheál and Hilton, and Shelah Richards. Others equally beloved in my memories include Jennifer Johnston, the writer, daughter of actress Shelagh Johnston and her playwright husband Denis. Their son Micheál is a director at RTÉ.

Lelia Doolan is the crazy genius who directed the best-ever production of Seán O'Casey's Easter uprising play *Plough and the Stars* for RTÉ. I was her floor manager. Shot in the O'Casey's slums of Dublin, it starred Kate Binchy, Clive Geraghty, Finnuala O'Shannon, Marie Keane and May Cluskey, with Barbara Brennan as little Mollser, the frail consumptive child.

Lona Moran was another RTÉ friend — a wonderful artist and designer. Lona's family owned the Moran's Hotel in Dublin. Every day I lunched *en famille* in the hotel dining room. I was Lona's painting assistant, due to my enforced abandonment as an actor at the Olympia Theatre.

It was a challenging job. Lona and I had to reproduce the West End scenery by Thursday because the original sets and furniture had gone off on the boat to Shaftesbury Avenue for the West End opening. "Jeremy, where's your paintbrush?" she asked, cheerily.

My job was to cajole Dublin's shops into lending substitute set dressing. I had a horse and cart for collections. My parents would come down to their furniture-less house — bare but for two complimentary tickets to a Binkie Beaumont pre-run at the Olympia Theatre.

And there's my beloved brother and sisters — Nigel, Naomi, Jacqui and Giselle — and all their wonderful spouses, children and grandchildren. I'm very lucky to love them all as they love me.

There was Patrick — Pat — Scott, the acclaimed painter and boyfriend of Pat McLarnon. They used to come to dinner at my aunts, Sheila and Carmel Leahy. Sheila and Carmel were friends of Micheál and Hilton's and both ladies worshipped 'The Boys' — Christopher Fitz-Simon wrote a great book of the same name. He and his wife, Anne Makower, were directors in the early days of RTÉ. Christopher had been an actor.

Brendan Neilan was RTÉ's casting director, recruited by Hilton. Brendan had stars at his fingertips. There was also the outrageous Alpho O'Reilly, Head of Design at RTÉ. I remember, the Director-General announcing, "Miss Chloe Gibson is leaving as Head of Drama. We hope she will be replaced by the Head of Drama in Radio, Mr Patrick P. Maguire."

Alpho wailed, "Oh dear God, not another old lady!"

There was Matthew Russell. He was the mentor of Sheelagh Fullerton at Trinity College, Dublin, in the Legal Department. I met Sheelagh when she was flat-sharing with *Jackanory* director Marilyn Fox in Hampstead. Sheelagh became a major support in my life, helping me to buy my house in Battersea with her legal expertise. The best of pals ever since.

And then there is Neil Hardie, my dearest pal, who lives round the corner with his partner, Greg. I met Neil at BOAC, while I was booking a flight somewhere. We chatted up. He asked me to his house for dinner with work friends Rosemary Watson and Jillian Somers. What a pair — they were party girls with a capital P! Rosemary and Jillian, and Neil, became enormous parts of my life.

The girls went on holiday to Majorca with my parents, Una and Jack — they loved them. Rosemary jumped into a puddle with girlish glee, drenching everyone. "Isn't this fun?" she cried.

It wasn't. They were all soaked.

The girls lived in a flat on Tulse Hill. Rosemary bemoaned, "It's sad living with you, Jillian. More than anything, more than anything! I wanted a baby!"

Jillian replied, succinctly, "There's already been a film on that subject,

Rosemary, and it wasn't very pleasant!"

They moved from Tulse Hill to a flat in Oaks Avenue, near Dulwich. Caroline Dawson called it 'Bloke's Avenue'. They gave great dinner parties, inviting actor pals such as Christopher Biggins, Norma Dunbar, Michael Staniforth and Caroline. Rosemary's agenda was to get us all as pissed as possible while Jillian cooked up a magnificent dinner.

We were so drunk we could hardly taste it.

I first met Norma Dunbar when she was Kanga in *Winnie the Pooh* at the Phoenix Theatre. Christopher Biggins played Pooh and Michael Staniforth was Tigger. I later cast Norma in *Rentaghost* and *Galloping Galaxies!* She was a great star of the music hall Players' Theatre, where she lustily sang *Daisy, Daisy*. Biggins, Stuart and I sang it at her funeral.

And then there's dear Geoffrey Norris. When he was the music critic at *The Times*, he asked me to accompany him to the Queen Elizabeth Hall on the South Bank for a musical recital; it was to be based on early South American Aztec laments.

The silence of the wait for the soloist to appear was broken by an explosion of cellophane behind us. Geoffrey rotated to gaze at two women — guiltily clutching an unopened box of Maltesers — and turned them to stone with a basilisk stare.

Finally, the soloist bounded onto the stage with her instrument, which consisted of strings attached to a gourd. She was wearing an ensemble seemingly inspired by Clint Eastwood's outfit in *A Fistful of Dollars* — albeit wearing a *tiny* stetson and espadrilles instead of spur-jangling boots. This ensemble was a hindrance to her performance from the start. Have you ever tried to play a stringed instrument in a pancho?

She began with a long tremolo note.

A crackle, followed by the rattle of Maltesers behind us was equally ominous.

The soloist then plunged into violent bow discords, accompanied by pizzicato pluckings — it was the most frightful row. Breathing heavily, she returned to the tremolo.

Suddenly, there came a godalmighty racket from behind us. The near-opened box of Maltesers had slipped from the woman's hands.

Frantic grapplings and hissed expletives ensued. The Queen Elizabeth Hall was a step-tiered auditorium, so the chocolate balls clattered onto the floor like machine-gun fire, before proceeding to roll loudly towards the stage. The slightest foot movement from the rest of the audience was met with the sound of crunching explosions.

Undeterred, Clint Eastwood scraped on.

Geoffrey was snotting and shaking. He staggered from his seat to the exit — accompanied by more crackles and pops — and slipped through the door to freedom. With the psychological reaction to having obliterated the recital setting in, he let rip with loud guffaws that echoed around the South Bank.

Mercifully, the soloist finished and the audience fled, after a ripple of applause — mainly aimed at the Malteser ladies for hugely enlivening the recital!

More names? There are loads.

And I'm sorry if I've left you out — but I'm sure you'll return!

Gazing out over Queensland in the Outback

Scene 14

Down under

Digressions over! Where was I? Ah, yes — BBC. Finishing the film of *Westminster Abbey* and meeting the great Stuart. Bob Block had sent in a new script. It was a comedy about space travel. He called it *Worlds Apart*. I didn't like the title — *Worlds Apart* sounded like alternatives discussing their sexual problems on Channel 4 at midnight. So, I called it *Galloping Galaxies!* instead.

Robbie Swales played the lead — a Superman lookalike and the captain of our spaceship. The rest of his crew were Nigel Cooke and Paul Wilce. The scripts were OK but it needed a central character. I went to see *2001: A Space Odyssey* — a great movie — where, thank you, Stanley Kubrick, our central character was found. Kenneth Williams would play SID, the spaceship's bossy computer: "Take your hands off my floppy discs!"

Kenneth was delighted with the job — mainly because he could do all his dialogue the day before shooting. Paul Graydon, the grams op, played in SID's lines during the recording. Kenneth, of course, still came to the studio. He loved the cast — particularly handsome Robbie Swales. "Oooh, what a *dish!*"

My old pal Niall Buggy played Murphy, a pirate space captain, bringing all the aplomb of the great Dublin Abbey Theatre technique to his villainy. *Galloping Galaxies!* ran for two years.

Then came my next professional hiatus — Edward Barnes was retiring! Out of his leaving cake jumped Anna Home, abandoning TVS to become the new Head of BBC Children's Programmes. Edward had appointed Trees Plummer-Andrews as Head of Children's Acquisitions. We were all back together again — Anna, Trees and me — in the same BBC department!

***

Anna sent me a new script called *Round the Twist*, a terrific read.

"It's fabulous!" I told her. I thought it was set in Scotland since it featured lighthouses and all that.

Anna said coyly, "Would you like to visit your sister?"

"Which one? I have three. Naomi, Jacqui and Giselle."

"Your sister in Australia." Giselle lived in Australia.

"What's that got to do with the script?"

"It's set in Australia! *Round the Twist*! I want you to go to Melbourne to work on the series. The BBC is going to invest in it. The producer is Patricia Edgar, the Head of the Australian Children's Television Foundation. I'm sure you will get on... I hope!"

Patricia Edgar had a formidable reputation — formidable with a capital 'f'.

I'd been to Australia before to see my sister, Giselle, her husband, Patrick and their son, Simon. They all lived on the Gold Coast. And on that visit, I dropped in on Perth. Actually, you don't drop in anywhere in Australia. It's so vast and amazing — strategy has to be applied for every journey. Mind you, Sheelagh Fullerton became a legend on her visit to Melbourne, when she went there and back in one day to have lunch with a friend in Perth.

My visit to Perth was to see Michael Marks, with whom Neil Hardie and I shared a house in Fulham back when I rejoined the BBC. Neil's airline connections got me upgraded to Business Class. Perth was a bit like Brisbane — no offence to either city — but Sydney was something else; that beautiful harbour with that extraordinary fantastical opera house!

The hotel concierge told me the Opera Theatre was meant to have been the Concert Hall and the Concert Hall was meant to be the Opera Theatre. Confused, I went to the box office to get a ticket for *The Marriage of Figaro*.

"Nah, sorry," sniffed the acerbic box office clerk. "The Mozart opera is totally booked out for the rest of its run." He took pity on my chagrin. "Nevertheless, there are seats for tonight's opera."

"Great! What's tonight's opera?"

"Tonight's opera is *The Gondoliers* by Gilbert and Sullivan."

"That's not an opera. it's an *operetta*."

"It's an opera here, dear!" he sneered. "I've got seats in the Gold Reserve and the Silver Reserve."

"What's the difference between the Gold Reserve and the Silver Reserve?"

"You can't hear anything in the Silver Reserve."

The Gondoliers at the Sydney Opera House was terrific. The seat in the Gold Reserve was perfect and inside, the Opera House was unbelievable. I thought it would be nice to relate my appreciation to the snappy box office clerk the next day. He was delighted and told me he had been a dancer, in *No, No, Nanette* at Drury Lane. My friend Thora Hird had been in that production, so this delightful showbiz bonding prompted him to ask me if I'd like to see a dress rehearsal of *Il Trovatore*.

"It's for the Friends of the Opera House. There's bound to be a seat," he

I saw these ladies in Melbourne's Chapel Street.
It was midday, so the contrast was highly acceptable

said, suggesting a paucity of Opera House friends.

"When is it?"

"Now! Rita Hunter sings the lead."

As I went to my seat, I heard a loud crash from behind the closed tabs. *What was that?* I sat down and next to me was an Australian friend I'd met years before in London, at Willie and Dorgan Rushton's flat — actor Bea Aston who had been married briefly to Christopher Biggins. Great reunion hoots followed. Bea was with Maggie Dence, a star of *Neighbours*.

The rehearsal was about to start. The house lights went down. And then the stage manager stepped through the curtains. Always a bad sign.

"Ladies and Gentlemen," he announced, "Miss Rita Hunter."

Intakes of breath and a few *"Oh, shits..."* were heard. Miss Rita Hunter was an English operatic dramatic soprano of some note.

"Miss Rita Hunter has unfortunately had a stumble in her dressing room." That explained the loud crash. "But she will sing the role of the lovely Leonora in a wheelchair and — if you could bear with her, dramatically — she will be unable to sip the poison from the ring in the last act."

With that, he stepped back through the curtain to raise it for the first act and begin the show. It was a rousing production by Elijah Moshinsky. At one point, he had the male chorus energetically loading muskets instead of bashing anvils.

A man jumped up a few seats in front of us, wearing an elaborate jacket with epaulettes fashioned like the Sydney Opera House. "Where, *oh where* are the anvils?" he wailed, loudly.

Shouts of "Sit down, you mad Pom!" followed.

The mad pom was George Mallard, a flamboyant hat designer and my neighbour from Battersea. He had moved to Australia.

Miss Rita Hunter was trundled on — the stage manager pushing her wheelchair — and timorously sang her first aria, while indicating with a bandaged finger. The mezzo-soprano playing Azucena came on and sang out very loudly and confidently. This was a vocal challenge to Leonora — who sang out louder and more confidently back. An epic rivalry.

On this first visit to Oz, Ann Emery had arranged for me to meet Joan Thorburn, the Mayor of Manly, and the first woman to hold that position. She was a great hostess. "Manly was named by the sailors of Captain Cook's ship when it sailed into Sydney Harbour," she told me. "They saw splendidly physiqued Aborigines on the beach. 'Hey, aren't those guys manly,' said a sailor to his mate on the poop deck. And that's how Manly got its name."

＊＊

A good introduction to Australia. And a welcome return. Back to the narrative — as I said, Anna Home asked me to go to Melbourne, to act as the BBC producer of *Round the Twist* and to work with Patricia Edgar. In Melbourne, the Australian Children's Television Foundation (ACTF) put me up in the Old Melbourne Hotel, a 15-year-old suburban hotel. On arrival, after an interminable flight, I rang Don Bennetts — having found his number in a telephone directory. He was very excited to hear from me.

"I'm coming round immediately!"

"Don't! I'm here on a job. From my third-floor window, I can see a crowd of people, all clutching folders displaying the ACTF logo, waiting for me in the lobby." The hotel had a horseshoe architecture. "I'll see you tomorrow."

I gathered my files. I was looking very BBC. Smart suit, white shirt and tie. Bit wobbly with the jetlag. I stood at the top of the stairs to the lobby... and then, unfortunately, fell arse over tit, all the way down, files flying.

Exclamations followed from the waiting crowd.

"Poor bastard!"

"He's pissed!"

"He's crook!"

I scrambled about gathering the files, picked myself up, smoothed my hair and announced, "I'm from the BBC!"

I couldn't have had a more fortunate introduction to the Australian Children's Television Foundation and the *Round the Twist* team. They were heartily amused by my spectacular entrance. 'They' were the great Patricia Edgar, the executive producer, Esben Storm, script consultant and director, Glenda Wilson, who was Patricia Edgar's secretary, Ewan Burnett, the associate producer, Elizabeth Symes, the production manager, Paul Jennings, the originator and writer of *Round the Twist*, and Peta Lawson, the production designer.

These were just a few of the wonderful crew I'd been sent to work with. I was to have a great time — the scripts were brilliant and the signature tune was phenomenal. It's still being sung by aficionados:

*"Have you ever, ever felt like this?
Have strange things happened?
Are you going round the twist?"*

When I tell people I worked on it, they immediately start singing — even my bank manager! It's an age indicator.

Paul Jennings created a great cast of characters. Actor Esben Storm was utterly dedicated to *Round the Twist*. He played Mr Snapper, the school head teacher, as well as directing. I took Patricia Edgar to my heart — along with her husband, Don and their daughters Lesley and Sue.

Anna was worried about how I was getting on in Australia. She needn't have been. Patricia and I had struck up a great friendship, which is still going strong. Anna and Patricia were powerful broadcasting ladies. I liked powerful broadcasting ladies and I encountered plenty: Shelah Richards, Chloe Gibson, Patricia Foy, Lelia Doolan, Biddy Baxter, Trees Plummer-Andrews and Monica Sims. Their dedication and devotion to their jobs was both vocational and inspirational — with just a *soupcon* of ruthlessness to keep everyone on their toes!

For months, it was backwards and forwards to Australia for the BBC on *Round the Twist*. Jet lag took on a new meaning.

"Can you come to Melbourne on Thursday?"

This was on Monday!

Staggering with jet lag, I was confronted with new storylines. One didn't grab me. The Australian team outlined the plot, in which the little boy, Bronson, saved a turtle's eggs.

"That doesn't grab me! The kids' audience in the UK isn't much into the preservation of turtles. Turtles are only acceptable in soup! Maybe another storyline, please?"

The jet lag had made me a bit terse. As I left the room, I overheard someone mutter "Pommy suck!" My lack of enthusiasm for the preservation of endangered turtles hadn't gone down well.

After a night of no sleep — jet lag again — I went into the ACTF HQ.

"We've got another storyline!" announced Esben Storm.

"Great! I'm sorry I didn't like the turtle one."

"No turtles. We're still focusing on the little boy, Bronson."

"Excellent! We like little boy stories at the BBC."

"Bronson is failing in a competition with his mates in the schoolyard."

"Marvellous! We love schoolyard competitions."

"He helps a water sprite from having its home dammed."

"Now we're really cooking on gas! Water sprites! A firm favourite!"

I was slightly over-egging my enthusiasm, to make up for the previous day's curtness and being branded a 'Pommy suck'.

"And, as a reward to Bronson for saving his watery home, the water sprite helps Bronson win the schoolyard competition over his mates."

"Terrific! The script is already leaping off the page. Write it! Write it! Write it!"

They all beamed at my reaction.

"By the way," I asked. "What's the competition that Bronson is having with his mates in the schoolyard — which the water sprite helps him win?"

A mischievous twinkling of Australian eyes.

"It's a who-can-pee-the-highest competition!"

Cripes.

"We're going to call it *Little Squirt*."

"I bet you are! Err... um... I think I'd better run the plot through with Anna Home. I'll phone her tonight."

I stayed up half the night in the Lygon Lodge motel to ring Anna. Time difference and all that jazz. I got through to the Beeb.

"Yes, it's all going fine, Anna. Er... um, what do you think of a who-can-pee-the-highest competition in *Round the Twist*?"

"A *what*?"

I repeated.

She paused a beat, then replied, "How do the girls fare?"

Little Squirt had all the naughtiness that first drew Anna to *Round the Twist*. It was excellently made, tastefully shot — no willies — and ended with a magnificent jet of water spouting up from the boys' toilet in the schoolyard. The episode won the Prix Jeunesse and went out to suitable fuss on BBC Children's Programmes.

I went to lunch with Stuart's parents in Surrey. His mother said, "You were mentioned on *Points of View* yesterday, Jeremy."

"OK, that's nice. Why the mention?"

"You were responsible for a programme about... about a competition in a school in Australia. It sounded very... rude!"

"Not in the least, Joyce!"

Paul Jennings stopped writing *Round the Twist* and so I was part of a group, assembled by Esben, to come up with new storylines. One episode featured a Viking ship, laden with behorned occupants, arriving on the coast of New South Wales. More hysterical than historical.

At the same time as these literary excursions to Melbourne, I was producing and directing back on home turf. *Bluebirds* was a series by Angela Ince and Shirley Lowe, about a pack of kids and their grannies forming a vigilante group to right the wrongs of the council block where they lived. The grannies were Barbara Windsor, Isabelle Lucas, Pauline Delaney and Sheila Steafel. I loved Barbara Windsor — Kenneth Williams had introduced us.

One great trick used by many ongoing TV series is to repeat the climax of the previous episode, which can help make up any timing deficiencies in the allotted slot. One *Bluebirds* episode ended on a knife edge with a baby girl in a runaway pram about to be struck by an approaching bus.

This tableau of impending doom, filmed on location, was witnessed by the grannies, sitting in a café built in the studio. "Don't worry!" yelled Mabel, played by Barbara Windsor. "I'll save her!"

With that, the show ended with Barbara running through the café door — well, as much as she could run in stilettos. Exciting stuff!

The next episode began with Barbara holding a dummy baby. We'd shot nail-varnished hands grabbing a baby from the pram, followed by the screeching of brakes and a terrible smash — with the pram rolling on its side into a gutter.

"I saved her!" said Barbara, heroically.

"Hold it!" I yelled at the rehearsal.

Robert Checksfield, our production manager on the floor, asked, "What's the matter?"

"The matter is that she goes out the door with a blonde wig and she's back with an auburn hairdo!"

"Ah. Barbara, darling," began Robert, soothingly. "A slight continuity problem."

"*Slight*?" I bellowed. She ran out blonde and she's come back auburn!"

Robert explained this implausibility to the star.

"Don't worry, Jeremy," she called up to the control room. "I'll solve it."

"How?"

"I'll improvise!"

We rehearsed the scene again. Barbara came running in — this time holding the dummy baby upside down.

"Oh, Mabel," declared the other grannies, "You saved her!"

"Yes, I did! She's OK now," said Mabel, straightening the baby the right way up. Then came the improvisation — Barbara touching her crowning glory with a spare hand. "By the way? Do you like the hair?"

The young girl in the *Bluebirds* kids' gang was played by Martine McCutcheon. She and Barbara went on to star in *EastEnders* — for which Barbara wore many changing wigs.

At the same time, I was taken on by Chris Bellinger as the director of *Going Live!*, the BBC's Saturday morning children's magazine show. Chris was the editor. I called it '*Going Dead*' because of the unearthly hour I had to turn up to direct on Saturday mornings — 5am! We went on the air at 7am with cartoons, during which I rehearsed pop groups for transmission at 9am.

Going Live! was presented by Phillip Schofield and Sarah Greene. They were superb presenters and a joy to work with. Sarah had been Aladdin for my big panto years earlier and Phillip was an accomplished presenter who went on to star in the theatre in *Joseph and the Amazing Technicolor Dreamcoat* and *Doctor Dolittle*.

Years later, when I was directing *Sooty* for Granada — back in Quay Street again — I went with Sue Nicholls to the Manchester Opera House to see Phillip in *Doctor Dolittle*. There was a flurry of excitement in the theatre when we arrived and Sue was recognised from *Coronation Street*. Great shouts of "Hi, Audrey!" followed us as we found our seats.

Later, at dinner, Phillip told us about his introduction to theatre. He'd gone to see Jason Donovan in *Joseph and the Amazing Technicolor Dreamcoat* at the London Palladium. There was teenage uproar when Phillip entered the theatre. Canny Andrew Lloyd Webber observed the adulation, "That's the guy to take over from Jason when he leaves."

"It was the audience's reaction that got me the part," explained Phillip.

"I hate to tell you, darling," Sue replied, "After tonight, I'm taking over as Doctor Dolittle!"

* * *

But back to Australia. I returned for *The Genie from Down Under*, a series created by Esben Storm and Patricia Edgar, following on from the success

IS THAT YOU, MAUREEN?

of *Round the Twist*. Patricia wanted me to direct a couple of episodes and to also be the associate producer. The BBC was putting money into it again — hence me!

I was too vain back then to admit that this was a bit too much for me to chew. The script was very complicated... flying carpets swooping under Sydney Harbour Bridge, huge scenes in the Outback — a nightmare! The Australian film crew worked to the highest standards of their craft — and expected the same qualities from the director.

Gulp.

I had great support from Esben and Patricia and the series producer, Phil Jones. And not a lot from the other executive producer, Peter Jackson at ABC (no, not the *Lord of the Rings* one) — but you can't win 'em all! Anna was the BBC exec.

Our writer Steve J. Spears came up with a great opening episode. An Australian genie and his young son emerge from an opal, rubbed by a young English aristocrat girl, Penelope. She, her mother and their housekeeper are whisked away to the Australian Outback. An English girl needed to be cast as Penelope. I engaged Angela Grosvenor, a UK casting director who was great at finding just-right kids.

Angela found her, Alexandra Milman from Canterbury in Kent.

Alex and her mother — as chaperone — were flown to Australia for the 13-episode shoot. Anna Galvin, an established and beautiful Oz actress was cast as Penelope's mother. The Australian casting director was Liz Mullinar. I got a brownie point for suggesting Monica Maughan to play the housekeeper; Andrew Morgan and Michael Kerrigan's agent, Richard Wakeley, had mentioned her to me back in the UK.

It was very difficult to find the right actor to play the key role of the genie. We had endless auditions in Melbourne, but sadly none were right. I hated auditions. It was always a heart-breaking process — but, sadly, the only way to do it.

Patricia Edgar had asked me to go and see *Amadeus* by Peter Shaffer in Her Majesty's Theatre while we were doing the London casting. On the day, she was unwell.

"Do you want to use the tickets?"

I did. I brought along Don Bennetts as a treat. *Amadeus* was terrific, with Barry Otto as a brilliant Salieri, and an equally brilliant young actor as Mozart, Rhys Muldoon.

The next day a recovered Patricia asked me, "How was *Amadeus*?"

"Fabulous, and I've found our Genie."

Rhys Muldoon got the lead in *The Genie from Down Under*.

The main location for the series was a ramshackle porched house, which had originally been the set for *The Flying Doctors*. It was way out in the Outback, near Wentworth in Victoria.

This whole area was besieged by a dreadful drought — good for our visuals but miserable for the locals with their cattle herds. My driver was a lady farmer whose cows had had to be moved to Gippsland, where the terrain was more fertile. The inhabitants prayed for rain — their prayers were answered. On the night before filming, it *poured* down. The next day, the area looked like Leicestershire in spring! Drat!

Wentworth was a sad town. It had been designated as the capital of Australia based on its gambling laws. They built a huge casino. Then the laws changed, and the capital intentions were transferred to Canberra. We all stayed in Wentworth's defunct casino. It was probably no coincidence they called the detention centre in *Prisoner: Cell Block H* Wentworth.

Wentworth was near Mildura, where Patricia Edgar's parents lived. Her father, Reg Etherington, had been the Mayor of Mildura. It was her parents' wedding anniversary during filming. I was invited, and it was lovely to see Patricia and Don's daughters, Sue and Lesley. I was later invited to Sue's wedding to Santo in Melbourne, celebrated with a party in the much-loved Mietta's Restaurant — part eatery, part arts venue... long gone.

There were many great restaurants in Melbourne. Stuart celebrated his birthday in Florentino's with Don, Christine and the Edgars. The bill came to the same amount as his flight to Oz!

Anyway, *The Genie from Down Under* did well in the TV ratings.

A costume design for Mustafa Pipi from Uncle Jack and Cleopatra's Mummy

Scene 15

Goosed

I'm going to ease up now. Few of you will have ever heard of the people I am writing about. I'll get back to the BBC. I'd written a series called *Julia Jekyll and Harriet Hyde*. Before that, there was *Uncle Jack...* written by Jim Eldridge. Uncle Jack was an eco-crusader and undercover agent for MI5. We did four series.

One of the problems with any ongoing children's TV show is that the children grow up. The little boys suddenly sound like Orson Welles and the girls develop into Pamela Anderson. Jim solved the problem. Uncle Jack had a posse of nieces and nephews, all ready to step into the shoes of their adulting cousins. Uncle Jack was played by Paul Jones. He had done a programme for me, a one-off musical called *Coronet Capers* with Elaine Delmar. He was still a pretty flamingo, having been a lead singer with Manfred Mann — just right for Uncle Jack.

Pieter Rogers was a distinguished drama producer and a great friend of Penelope Keith's, who wore a fright wig — Pieter, not Penny. He rang me, having read the proposed *Uncle Jack* series and suggested that it needed a central villain down the Cruella de Vil road. A ruthless, evil woman, capable of extreme cunning utter cruelty and devilish machinations... and could he recommend a friend who had all the appropriate qualifications? Fenella Fielding. So the Vixen became Uncle Jack's arch enemy. Fenella was terrific — tricky, but terrific. The costume designer and the make-up supervisor nearly committed suicide!

"That Fenella Fielding has great cheek!" Kenneth Williams once told me. "We were getting ready for a take in *Carry on Screaming* and I had to sit on her lap. She moaned, 'Why is your bum so cold? Do you leave it out at night?'"

I was dubbing one series of *Uncle Jack* in which the Vixen had somewhat exceeded her artistic temperament. I was making sinister decisions in the suite. "Feast your eyes on her, boys," I grimly told my technical colleagues, "She's out!"

"Oh, no!" they all wailed. "We love her!"

"She always asks how my mother is!"

"She brought me an apple in the studio!"

"She sent make-up tips to my wife!"

Said wife visited the studio one day, looking like Danny La Rue.

"You've got to have her back or else!"

A golden rule for a TV director is to never upset the technicians. They run the show.

A phone call followed.

"Hi, Fenella, we're doing another series of *Uncle Jack* and I'd dearly love the Vixen to return."

She was delighted. "It would be a *pleasure*, darling. What's this series called?"

"*Uncle Jack and the Dark Side of the Moon*."

"How *thrilling!*" she purred. "Tell me, what ghastly creature is lurking on the dark side of the moon?"

"You are!"

Jim wrote a good script. The Vixen sat in a spaceship on the dark side of the Moon, holding the world's weather to ransom.

"Let me show you the powers of my command," she told the quaking PM (a John Major lookalike played by Christopher Owen) as she blasted the windows of 10 Downing Street to smithereens with a lightning strike. All Fenella had to do was press a button. And never was a button ever pressed so magnificently!

Episode six of *The Dark Side of the Moon* was titled *Off With His Head*. The script demanded that the Vixen appear as Elizabeth I. Wardrobe got the frock that Glenda Jackson wore in the BBC series playing the same.

"Darling, you look wonderful!" exclaimed Vivian Pickles, who also appeared in the show. "You really should be on the front of *Radio Times*."

Fenella gave a wry grin. "I think, Vivvie, the dress already has been!"

Elizabeth I appeared in the script's school play. She was to knight Paul Jones' character Uncle Jack as Sir Francis Drake, with the intention of chopping off his head. Of course, she was thwarted, to save the hero for the next series, *Uncle Jack and Cleopatra's Mummy*. Fenella, as the Vixen, appeared variously as the reincarnation of Elizabeth Taylor, Pola Negri and Claudette Colbert as Cleopatra. She was a villain supreme.

On *Cleopatra's Mummy*, I was a bit peeved when I heard that the art department, plus wardrobe, had flown off to Cairo for 'research'. But the budget was justified by great sets and fabulous costumes, purchased in the Souk. Another lovely cast — Paul Jones, Tricia George, Moyra Fraser, Caroline O'Connor, Natasha Gray, Patrick Marley and Roger Hammond. At the recommendation of Vivian Pickles, I cast Stewart Permutt as a browned-up Arabian restauranteur, Mustafa Pipi. Of course, you can't brown up actors anymore — now you've got to find a real Mustafa Pipi.

At rehearsal, Stewart said to me, "Can I suggest a dialogue exchange?"

That never went down well.

"What?" I asked, coldly.

"Well, when I escort the American ambassador to his table, can I say, 'Walk this way'?"

"*And*?"

"And then the American ambassador says, 'If I walked that way, I'd be arrested!'"

I shot the dialogue exchange down in flames.

Roger Hammond was in all the *Uncle Jack*s as M — no relation to Q. He was a dear cast additive. Everyone adored him. He was lovable, delightful and sympathetic to all. He told me that he'd been at the deathbed of John Saunders, a fellow actor. "Darling Johnny. He was gently slipping away. I held his hand and murmured in his ear, 'Dearest, darling Johnny, go in peace, and... and... can I buy your car?'"

※ ※ ※

A digression down the villain road... Back to 1976, when I was arrested in Darlington, County Durham! Christopher Biggins was *Mother Goose* in Darlington Civic Theatre's panto. I went up there and joined Christopher, his parents, Pam and Bill, and his little brother Sean. Christopher put us all up in a posh hotel. He was a fantastically wonderful Dame — a role he was to repeat for decades all over the country.

The day after the panto triumph, Pam, Bill, Sean and I were deposited at Darlington Station for the return trip to London. They were going back home to Salisbury. There were goodbyes to the waving Christopher. Pam wanted to buy a copy of *Woman's Own* at the platform's paper shop. Bill wanted *The Times*, Sean wanted Smarties. The London train was to leave in 20 minutes. Bags of time.

"Put the cases on the train, Jeremy," I was instructed by Pam Biggins. "Find seats for four and we'll all join you."

I put the cases on the train. 18 minutes to spare. I was no sooner on the train with the cases when there was a starting jolt. Dear God — the train was pulling out! Mrs Biggins raced from the newsagent and did a *Doctor Zhivago* run along the platform.

"Throw out the bags! Throw out the bags!" she shrieked.

I obeyed. One case exploded on the platform — knickers, pyjamas and the rest, billowing in the draft from the departing train. It suddenly jerked to a shrieking halt. I was on the carriage platform at an open door. Police appeared from everywhere.

"Would you mind coming with us, sir?"

"The train has left 18 minutes early!"

"No, it hasn't — it's the Flying Scot from Glasgow, running ten minutes late! Would you mind accompanying us to the station office on the platform?"

In the station, a severe interrogation followed. My Irish accent made the police very suspicious. The IRA was at its height on the mainland.

"What are you doing in Darlington, sir?"

"I'm here to see *Mother Goose*."

"What?"

Mother Goose burst into the station.

"He's innocent" he bawled.

"Nevertheless, we are charging Mr Swan with obstructing the schedule of the Flying Scot, throwing objects from a moving train, endangering lives like the poor woman gathering up her smalls on the platform. So, we're charging him."

"This is outrageous!" yelled Christopher.

"Nevertheless, Mother Goose, we are charging him."

With a summons in my grasp, we all boarded the train. Biggins waved us away again — written all over his face, the relief of 'Thank God they're off!'

"Don't worry, Jeremy," Bill said, as the train chugged out of Darlington.

Sean piped up. "Is Jeremy going to go to prison?"

"Any more remarks like that, young Sean, and I'll belt you one!" I snapped.

Pam sniffed. "That's right. Add child molestation to your other charges."

Back at the BBC, Monica Sims asked, "Did you have a nice Christmas?"

"Terrific — I got arrested in Darlington." I related the saga.

That was not the end. Months later, the long arm of the law reached from Darlington to my home in Battersea, when a summons arrived on my doormat. I could plead not guilty and therefore appear in court. Or plead guilty and pay a fine. I opted for the latter.

A permanency position occurred for my job at the BBC. "There's a snag," said Mr Perkins, the personnel officer. "You've got a police record, arrested in Darlington."

"I paid the fine!"

Luckily — very luckily — I'd told Monica of my escapade. She waived aside any obstacle.

"Well, that's Jeremy! He's dodgy, but he's not a criminal."

*A Christmas card design for Ann Emery,
at the time appearing in* Billy Elliot The Musical

Scene 16

Raised sets

That last digression was ages ago. Hot on the heels of *Uncle Jack*, at the BBC we were all offered redundancy packages — they wanted to get rid of us! All very sinister. Envelopes were delivered. I put mine at the bottom of the pile. I'd been told I was too busy to apply.

Meanwhile, I had another overseas assignment. On the strength of my work on *Fraggle Rock*, I was back with the Henson Company again, to direct *The Secret Life of Toys*. I'd had a whisper of this when I was assigned to work on a puppet series being filmed in Spiddal, County Galway. Not a big job — I was just there to put the oar in, if required, wielding a bit of BBC clout. Jocelyn Stevenson was also there as writer and producer, a brilliant loan from the Henson Organisation. She told me about their interest in me for *The Secret Life of Toys*.

The Spiddal puppetry was produced by O Telefis, a now-extinct Irish-speaking TV company. I can't remember the name of the show but was a great idea, centred around a mermaid. One puppeteer worked the body, another worked the tail. It was first made in Irish, then in Basque, Welsh, Cornish, Erse and some other obscure European language. The obscurity ensured hefty government grants for nationalistic promotion. Luckily, puppets speak in flap-flap, so are easily dubbable. Stuart joined me after the shoot, coming from staying with my parents in Dublin. We motored around magnificent Connemara in County Galway and nearly met our end as a storm lashed the cliffs of Moher, in County Clare.

The Secret Life of Toys was to be shot in Germany. Michael Kerrigan was assigned as a second director. He was a great pal from my early *Jackanory* days. Off we went to Cologne — the studios were outside the city in Monheim. The show was about the toys coming alive after the kids went to bed. Before their mother summoned them to sleep, the children set up the toys for the episode's situation. For example, the teddy bear might be the King, the pretty doll, Daffodil, the Queen, the humble tiger toy a serf and the rag doll the maid. Upon coming alive, the rag doll bashed Daffodil's head off in a jealous fit, thus giving us the plot — to get the head back on. Jocelyn Stevenson wrote terrific scripts. Decapitation is always a winner.

The producers were Pete Coogan, Martin G. Baker and Brian Henson, son of Jim. Anna was the BBC exec, along with Trees Plummer-Andrews. There was a hugely talented puppet team — Dave Goeltz and Jerry Nelson from the New York Creature Shop, Louise Gold and Nigel Plaskitt from the UK, plus puppetry pillars from *Spitting Image* Mike Quinn.

A big set was built in the Monheim Studios for the attic playroom of the toys. It was about two metres high with removable squares on steel pillars in the raised floor, which went in and out for the puppets' 'runs'; the squares that remained were the background and foreground floor.

You might think it's tricky working with actors — by God, try working with puppets! The shooting was dominated by the Creature Shop team, who scrutinised every shot. Paul Hartis from New York was in charge of that. The initial rehearsals were done with the puppeteers holding up their hands and flapping their fingers against thumbs. They sat on wheely office chairs, paddling with their feet. The floor sections were moved in and out as required. Monitors were strapped to the puppeteers' chests so they could see the shot, along with mics for the dialogue. The first week, working from 8am till 6.30pm, we filmed only two and a half minutes!

"Things will speed up," said the experienced puppeteers, trying to calm my nervous breakdown.

We were put up in Cologne's luxurious Hyatt Hotel on the banks of the Rhine. On my arrival in my room, 204, I vainly tried to turn off the incessant irritating muzak. Somewhat forcibly, I tugged away at knobs and buttons. The entire pseudo-marble bedhead came away and the bed up-ended! I rang room service. Two Turkish maids appeared, surveyed the wreckage and muttered to each other in Turkish something that roughly translated as, "What the *fuck* has happened here?"

I was moved to another room, minus muzak.

Stuart had given me an elasticated type of clothesline with adhering hooks, so I could dry my smalls at the hotel. In the bathroom of the new room, I put it to the test, hooking it onto glass shelves and the shower door. I rinsed my pyjamas, drip-dry shirts, briefs and socks in shampoo. I draped the dripping sodden mass on Stuart's line, closed the door and went to read my script on the bed.

There was the most appalling crash.

The laden line had ripped off the glass shelves and the shower door in a shattering explosion! I rang for room service. The same Turkish maids appeared and recoiled when they opened the bathroom door. One said to the other something in Turkish, which roughly translated as, "It's the motherfucker from 204!"

* * *

The schedule was arranged so that I'd direct one week and Michael would direct the next. The somewhat limited technical facilities of the studio meant that the post-production machines were tied up recording during the day, so editing would ensue after the day's shooting. Editing was from 6.30pm till God-knows-when in the morning before 8.30am when they were needed again. So one director came in as the other went out.

Andrew Morgan was also in Cologne, directing a cop thriller, *Die Wache,* which was German TV's answer to *The Bill.* We met for dinner — Michael, Andrew and me.

"I've had a really busy day," Andrew told us. "Four prostitutes had to jump off the bridge into the Rhine to be hauled aboard a gangster speed boat, then police motorboats pursued them up the river. We had to close the Rhine and the helicopter camera nearly crashed into the Kölner Dom! It was frightful!"

"We had a frightful day too."

"Oh, really? Doing what?"

"A mouse running up and down a curtain."

As you'll gather, we were able to duck away from editing, leaving it to Maria, our clever Spanish editor. To say the production was multilingual would be an understatement! I liked the mix of languages, particularly the German word 'probe' for rehearsal.

Michael's family, his wife Jane, and his very young daughter and son, Chloe and Richard, came for a visit — and Anna Home came down from a conference in Amsterdam. Distance was nothing for Anna!

At the end of the very long shoot, the puppets were sadly laid to rest in their boxes, never to emerge. I wanted to do another series; it was very popular and I was nominated for an Emmy, but we were gazumped by the other co-producer, Disney, who of course made *Toy Story*.

***

From *The Secret Life of Toys*, I was sent to direct *The Genie from Down Under* in Australia. I've already told you about that. Before I left for foreign climes, I submitted *Julia Jekyll and Harriet Hyde* to Anna, making no apology to Robert Louis Stephenson. It was about a schoolgirl who turned into a monster — played by John Asquith in a hulking costume. I wrote twelve episodes, which went down well.

Ann Emery and Simon Greene played a mother and son running a chaotic school — the Rocket Academy. A wonderful group of kids, found by Angela Grosvenor, made up the main cast. Olivia Hallinan as Julia Jekyll was a great find and has become a very fine actress.

Anna wanted more episodes so I brought in Jim Eldridge to help write the scripts and Albert Barber joined me as a director. We did 53 episodes. Such is the appetite of television. I thought Julia Jekyll should have a little pal, whom Mr Rocket introduced to the students at the school assembly.

"The new boy does have a weak spot — his surname. He's very sensitive about it. Now, the Rocket Academy has always distinguished itself with unusual surnames. There are Rockets, Jekyll, Blisters..."

A pause for effect. "And now there will be Knickers. Edward Knickers!"

Guy Edwards, who we cast as Edward, went on to play the title role in *The Winslow Boy*, a great film. When he left, I replaced him with another little boy, Steven Webb, who went on to a long, long run in *The Book of Mormon*. They were a splendid pair of Knickers.

Ann Emery, who played *Julia Jekyll*'s Mrs Rocket, was a wonderful actress and a darling friend. She had been in *Rentaghost* as Mrs Meaker and was a stalwart of many West End musicals, including *Cats* and *Martin Guerre*. Ann taught Wayne Sleep how to tap dance. She taught me to drive. Friends I'd driven said, "I'm not surprised!"

Billy Elliot The Musical, was having difficulty casting Billy's grandmother. Director Stephen Daldry and composer Elton John saw every old trout in Equity. Ann had gone for an audition of *Mary Poppins* to sing *Feed the Birds* at Drury Lane. Sadly, Cameron MacIntosh didn't pick her. Bitterly, she went to audition for Grandma in *Billy Elliot* at the Victoria Palace. She was very good.

"You were very good," said the genial Stephen Daldry. "We'll give you a recall."

Ann replied, "If I was that bloody good, why give me a bloody recall?"

Daldry was smooth.

"That's the way it works, Miss Emery."

She gave him the two fingers and stomped off the Victoria Palace stage.

"Well, really!" expostulated the production team. "What a cheek!"

"We'll have to have another nationwide search," declared Stephen Daltry.

"We've already had a nationwide search," wailed his colleagues.

After more auditions, clever Stephen Daldry said, "I know who's right."

"Who?"

"Ann Emery."

"But she gave us the two fingers and told us to piss off!"

They came up with a plan. They'd ask Ann, who lived nearby in Pimlico, to come in and help out with the little Billys — feed them lines, to help their performances. And thereby, Mr Daldry could have a closer look at her. Ann was agreeable. After all, she'd do anything to help a production. So she got on the Number 24 bus to Victoria. She cued little Billys on the stage. Stephen Daldry ventured onto thin ice.

"Maybe, Miss Emery, to help the boys, you could try a Newcastle voice?"

The cuing continued.

"Oh no! That's Scottish!" Ann cried. "I'll try again! No, no! That's Chinese! No, that's Irish!"

The little boys were laughing their heads off — so were Stephen Daldry and Elton John.

Our mutual agent, Paul Spyker, called me.

"Have you heard from Ann?"

"No. She hasn't committed suicide after *Feed the Birds*, has she?"

"She's bound to call you."

I knew nothing about the *Billy Elliot* exploration. Ann did indeed call, to tell me that she had got the Grandma part. She was so excited. "I'm sending a telegram to Cameron MacIntosh, telling him to feed his own bloody birds!"

Ann sent my agent Paul Spyker and me tickets for the first night at the Victoria Palace. The show was wonderful, and so was Ann. We went round at the end to her dressing room.

"How was I?" she asked us, nervously, defoiling a bottle of Bollinger.

She knew how she was! We let rip with unanimous praise. There was a knock on the door. I opened it. Outside were Stephen Daldry and Elton John, *salaaming* on their knees, saying to Ann, "Thank you! Thank you!"

She was in *Billy Elliot* for ten years as Grandma.

At her memorial service in St Paul's Covent Garden, the Actors' Church, Haydn Gwynne — who starred alongside Ann as the dance teacher Mrs Wilkinson — organised all old Billys and miners to sing *Solidarity*, the great *Billy Elliot* anthem. Anna Home said it was the best send-off ever.

Meanwhile, my redundancy package was looming at the BBC. I was doing OK. *Julia Jekyll and Harriet Hyde* was No 1 in *Broadcast* magazine and slammed by the *Daily Mail* as camp crap.

Well, maybe not those exact words, but who reads the *Daily Mail*?

A too-dominant Attavanti, painted for Christopher Biggins' Tosca

Scene 17

'My object all sublime'

Christopher Biggins rang me. "I'd like you to direct *The Mikado*."
"Oh, no, Christopher, I can't! The BBC would never permit it."
"In Barbados?"
"I'll run it by Anna."
"Anna, Christopher Biggins has asked me to direct *The Mikado*."
"Well, you can't. Where?"
"In Barbados."
"How wonderful! You must!"

Good ol' Anna! She loved the idea of me doing something like that. She added, "You can use your annual leave."

Christopher rang me from the Caprice restaurant, his favoured celeb hangout. "How's *The Mikado*?"
"I've listened to the fucking thing till I'm deaf!"
"Great, the designs have to be in Barbados. I'm going there tomorrow."
"I've very clear ideas of how it should look. Who's the designer?"
"I forgot to tell you — you are! Can you get sketches down to me by 11pm at the Caprice?"

I worked like a maniac at my kitchen table. The production was to be staged in the open air. So, I designed a cruise ship — Barbados was big on cruise ships — with a gangplank for the cast to go up and down on.

I got a taxi to the Caprice.

"Brilliant!" Just what I wanted!" exclaimed Christopher, and shoved the designs in his pocket.

I'd been to Barbados before with Neil Hardie, Rosemary Watson and Jillian Somers... was it back in 1969? They were all able to go BOAC (later British Airways) — staff travel cheapo, I had to pay full whack. Barbados was paradise on earth. We'd rented a house in Sunset Crest.

A good wheeze for *social entrée* was for the four of us to stroll along the beach in the evening, looking elegant. Upon hearing the sound of revelry, Jillian would push through the oleander hedge and dive into the swimming pool, fully clothed and shrieking with gay laughter. The party guests would applaud such bravura while the rest of us slithered through the hedge, grabbing drinks from passing butlers — everyone was very rich in Barbados).

I'd been smarting from the load of dosh I'd paid to get there, but I had the last laugh. When the time came for us to depart, Neil, Rosemary and

My design for the ship set

Jillian were off-loaded! That meant the flight home was full. That meant no staff travel, so they had to wait for the next available flight that had space to take staff. That meant I got on to my paid, booked seat to the UK — while they ended up in Montevideo, Uruguay, before two days later attempting to get on a BOAC flight to Heathrow.

***

Moving on... Set designs were delivered to Christopher — a few costume sketches also had to be included. Jeannie Mandray, who had a rag-trade business in Mortimer Street, would supply the fabrics for the cossies; she was a great pal of Biggins. Also appearing in our Barbados repertoire were productions of *Tosca*, *Twelfth Night* and a Sondheim evening and cabaret. Christopher, as well as serving as overall artistic director, was directing *Tosca*. I was a bit jealous, preferring Puccini's melodies to the *oom-pah-pah* of Gilbert and Sullivan.

"*Tosca*'s tricky," I warned him. "There's that big *Te Deum* at the end of Act 1."

"I know," said Christopher. "I haven't cast her yet."

We all assembled at the Welsh Centre at Gray's Inn Road for the start of three weeks of rehearsals. Christopher had a dental operatic expert, Walter J. Reid, to guide him through the complexities of Puccini: Nichola McAuliffe was directing *Twelfth Night* alongside them with a lethal CIA approach; Stephen Sondheim was in the capable hands of the musical director, Peter Crockford. The stage management was handled by Maris Sharp and her assistant, the very young Brad Fitt. Witnessing the intensities of Puccini and Shakespeare, I could see that Gilbert and Sullivan were not going to get much of a look-in at the rehearsals!

Rosemary Wagner Scott — niece of Robert Wagner — was playing Tosca. Robin Green was Cavaradossi. Denis Quilley was Sir Toby Belch in *Twelfth Night* with Berwick Kaler as Malvolio and Liz Robertson as Olivia. A brilliant Welsh singer, Terence Sharpe, was Scarpia in *Tosca*. Disabled, he played it on crutches, which added menace and terror to the role.

The producer for the season was Johnny Kidd, assisted by his wife Wendy and Richard Hanlon. The Kidds lived in Barbados in Holders House and the theatrical festival was to be held on a knoll — a little hill — in Johnny's polo field. The 1995 season had been very successful, hence why he had asked Christopher back the following year, with me in tow.

Christopher had been a part of my life for a very long time. I first met him in my early *Jackanory* days and loved him ever since. You could describe Christopher as a life enhancer. Many stars will endorse his entry into their firmament!

There were 91 of us in the company, including the Wren Orchestra. My *Mikado* cast was Stefan Bednarczyk as the Mikado, Nichola McAuliffe as Katisha, Kit Hesketh-Harvey as Pooh-Bah, Richard Sisson as Pish-Tush, Rosemary Ashe as Yum-Yum, Liz Robertson as Pitti-Sing, Cory Pulman as Peep-Bo, Edward Baker-Duly as Nanki-Poo and Paul J. Medford as Ko-Ko. He was a star of *EastEnders* and had a lot of Barbadian

Rosie Ashe enlisted a choreographer — quite right, too, I was incapable of such talent. Kenn Oldfield realised all my directorial intentions, coming up with perfect routines.

All of us flew to Barbados. It was a hell of a movement. Accommodation was dotted around little hotels and digs from obliging locals. Christopher and I stayed in the providentia of the Contessa Karla Cavalli. A providentia is a residence for guests, adjacent to the big house. A couple of other contessas were rattling around — guests of Karla and her companion, Theo Rossi, who owned Martini & Rossi, the big booze company.

Christopher and I shared a vast suite. Sleep was difficult for me with Christopher snorting, sneezing and snoring from the other side of the room. So I pushed my bed into the enormous walk-in wardrobe and slept blissfully under Christopher's billowing laundered shirts.

I woke the next morning to yelling and shouts from Christopher.

"He's been kidnapped! And what's worse, they've pinched the bed!"

* * *

My set was built — the gigantic ship. But it had been painted an alarming shade of pastel blue.

"It's meant to be dark green!"

"Sure, man, but de green ain't goin' stand out! All roun' it is dark green under de trees. Get wid it, man."

"I am *wid* it! We'll repaint it — dark green!"

I got a lift into Bridgetown and found the paint department of Cave Shepherd, the capital's big shop. They mixed the right colour and I stood outside with the large tins, wondering how I was going to haul them back to Holders House and the pastel-blue ship. Gloria Hunniford pulled up in a moke and sweetly offered me a lift — everyone was in Barbados. We nearly ran over Pavarotti on the way back, while narrowingly missing Cliff Richard. Barbados was known as *Hello!*-on-Sea.

Gloria's daughter was Caron Keating. I knew her from *Blue Peter* and she was a neighbour back in Battersea. Caron once came to supper *chez moi* with Caroline Dawson.

"She is the most beautiful girl," Caroline said.

She was — and so tragically taken from us all, far too young. I told Caron's mother how I loved her daughter. That was a bond.

Back at the ranch, there was much slathering of dark green over the pastel blue — with the giggling assistants all high on Ganja, the local recreational smoke. One of them knocked over one of my cans and dark green seeped into the parched ground. I was hopping mad. He took me on the back of his motor scooter to Cave Shepherd and balanced a new tin on his rasta hat for the journey back to Holders House.

Steven Gregory, the costume guy, sought me out.

"The material bales have arrived from Jeannie Mandray."

"Excellent. Start cutting and stitching."

"You'd better have a look."

I made a call to Jeannie Mandray, back in London.

"Hi Jeannie, the bales have arrived OK."

"Excellent, darling. Are you pleased?"

"Er... Jeannie. What's with all the gingham?"

"Perfect for your show, darling."

"Eh — what's my show?"

"*Oklahoma!*"

"Jeannie, it's *The Mikado*! Set in ancient Japan!"

"No problem, Jeremy. Simply border the cossies with a wide black satin ribbon and they're Japanese! Simple!" A pause. She clutched at a straw. "The Japanese invented gingham!"

Steven Gregory created some great costumes. Luckily, I had packed an elaborate black silk kimono — a present from Vanya.

Why had I? Maybe it was a premonition.

"Paul Medford can wear my kimono as Ko-Ko," I announced.

While I dark-greened, Kenn Oldfield was setting routines. Elsewhere, all the other productions were being rehearsed with whatever actors they could grab. Nichola was busy grabbing and directing *Twelfth Night*, while *Tosca* was ensconced with the Wren Orchestra under Peter Crockford.

As with all on-stage dramas, there were backstage dramas. Stewart Permutt, who was to be a walk-on for my show, had a wobbly. He was sharing a room with Brad in the barracoons at the back of Holders House. If you're unwell or disturbed, Brad Fitt is the best and most sympathetic companion you could ask for.

Christopher came to me. "I know you're a bit busy with *The Mikado*," — a huge understatement! — "but can you do the painting of the Attavanti for Act I of *Tosca*? Cavaradossi is meant to be painting it. It's only titchy, you'll knock it off very quickly!"

I remembered the *Tosca* plot. The painting of the Attavanti is *not* titchy! It's a major focal point in Act I. Brad arranged for a big prepared canvas to be delivered at Holders House; again, luckily, I'd packed my paints along with the kimono from Vanya.

Brad asked, "Can you do the painting in our room, to keep Stewart Permutt, who's having a nervous breakdown, company?"

Though not the artistic motivation of Cavaradossi, I agreed. Stewart was not at all well but my work suitably distracted him.

"Maybe a bit more yellow, Jeremy?"

"Take another pill, Stewart!"

I finished the huge picture of Tosca's envy and delivered it to the opera rehearsal.

"It's too dominant, Jeremy," declared the director.

Oh, for heaven's sake! But he was right, so I stippled the background with coffee dregs dipped in my bathroom sponge. I certainly wasn't going to get the paints out again.

* * *

Christopher had put together a wonderful production for *Tosca*. The set was a very tall red cross set up on the knoll, which worked for Act I's Church of Sant'andrea della Valle. He draped a rich brocade over it for Scarpia's Act II study; sumptuous fabric supplied by Jeannie Mandray — not gingham! Then he put the cross on its side, which worked as the crenellated turrets of Act III's Castel Sant'Angelo. Our performing knoll was below the kid's swimming pool, allowing Tosca to run up the steps

'MY OBJECT ALL SUBLIME'

A tableau design for The Mikado's *second act*

and dramatically throw herself into the mattressed, drained pool.

At the dress rehearsal, all the firing squad held up their guns to shoot Cavaradossi — except one. Our heroine, Rosemary Wagner Scott, ran up the steps to throw herself to her doom.

She sang out, "Scarpia! We shall meet on High."

The soldier fidgeted with his non-fired gun. Suddenly, it went off with a big bang! As she jumped, it looked as if Tosca had been shot in the back! Nevertheless, that's what dress rehearsals are for.

In my non-existent spare time, I busied myself painting the lyrics of *My Object All Sublime* on white parasols. I wanted a sing-along for the show's big number, dividing the audience into Katisha's team and the Mikado's team. Gilbert and Sullivan purists blanched, but then we were on a hillock in the middle of the Caribbean.

There were lots of parties. The first one was in the Contessa Karla Cavalli's house — a glittering affair. The next night's party was in another contessa's island palazzo. Another great time was had — all the people who had been at the party the night before were at this one. They just went *en masse* from party to party. It was the same entertainment every night — topped off by watching the optical illusion of the sun rippling into the so-called 'green flash', just before it sank below the horizon.

"This is what we do," the Contessa Marzia de' Medici said to me.

"Look at the green flash?"

"No, Caro. Feed each other!"

***

Christopher asked me to play the cardinal in *Tosca*, during the *Te Deum* hymn at the end of Act 1. The mitre came down to my chin, so we settled for an inauthentic skull cap. I made a monstrance out of two saucepan lids, with wire coat hangers to hold it aloft.

Dress rehearsal fever set in. I was very nervous about *The Mikado*. Most of the cast were pissed on rum punches at the dress run, but not the dependable Bajan gospel singers. They were magnificent.

"It had better improve for the opening," said Christopher, ominously.

It did, after an appropriate bollocking.

The glamorous first night finally arrived. A minuscule flaw occurred as the audience filed in. The sound guy had miked up the cast — the mics were live. Rosie Ashe's voice rang out over the speakers. "If he thinks I'm wearing these hen's-bum knickers under my gym slip, he can bloody think again! They make my arse look like an avalanche!"

Brad rushed backstage. A lot of crackles followed.

The overture started. Gilbert and Sullivan overtures are very long. Good, but long. Biggins turned to me in the production box. "When is this bloody thing going to start?"

At one rehearsal, the male chorus leader had taken me aside.

"Mr Swan, we're very worried."

"What are you worried about?"

"We're worried about pigtails and yellow faces."

"Oh, for God's sake! You're not to worry. No pigtails. No yellow faces!"

"But we sing, 'Do you want to know who we are? We are gentlemen of Japan.' How will they know we are gentlemen of Japan?"

"Under the flaps of your smartest shirts, out of your white trousers, you'll produce instamatic cameras. On the musical breaks, you'll take flash snaps of the audience!"

That solved that problem. I put aside the thought that some audience members might have epileptic fits as a result.

The lady chorus leader also came to me. The chorus consisted of large local ladies who were brilliant church gospel singers.

"Mr Swan, we're very worried!"

"What's the matter, darling?"

"The gangplank which we have to come down. And wearing little gym slips!"

"You don't have to come down the gangplank. You'll wear your prettiest dresses and come through the audience, waving fronds of bougainvillaea, stripped from Mr Kidd's hedges. You'll all be beautiful."

They were. And so were the handsome camera-flashing men.

No one had an epileptic fit.

The overture ended. The lights went up on the dark green ship, sparkling with strips of bacofoil representing cabin windows. The men's chorus came down the gangplank — thankfully no one slipped — and engulfed the audience in Gilbert and Sullivan's masterpiece.

I was very pleased, and so was Christopher. "I knew you wouldn't let us down," he beamed.

"You didn't say that at the dress rehearsal!"

* * *

Romance was in the air. Nichola McAuliffe was to marry her fiancé, Don MacKay, a distinguished journalist. Christopher had arranged for a glossy magazine to do a photoshoot of fashion models posing with characters from the productions. Beautiful girls in fab frocks draped themselves around the Mikado and Scarpia. In the collection was a fabulous wedding dress. Christopher had the kindest thought and gifted it to Nichola for her forthcoming nuptials.

This donation did not go down at all well with Don, her Scottish fiancé. "Are you insinuating, Mr Biggins, that my bride-to-be would be too *mean* not to buy her own wedding dress?"

The slur 'mean' is anathema to your average generous Scot, and evokes a justifiable Celtic ire — often with lethal intent. The ire manifested itself like a volcanic eruption in Don MacKay.

That evening we were all going out for a Viennese evening on the *Jolly Roger* — a gentle cruise around the calm Caribbean side of the island; the Atlantic side was wild and tempestuous, so the *Roger* would not have been so jolly! Brad and I sauntered along the balmy deck while the Wren Orchestra sawed away with gems from Strauss and Lehar. We were jostled by Don MacKay thundering past us.

"Was that a machete?" asked Brad.

We continued our stroll when we heard a faint tapping from a broom cupboard. Inside was a quaking Christopher.

"He's going to kill me!" he wailed, before scurrying off in the opposite direction to Don. The pursuit continued round the decks, accompanied by Viennese melodies till a firm Nichola put a stop to it.

The pursuit, not the melodies.

The wedding was lovely. Nichola looked wonderful in a vintage wedding dress — her own — and was photographed for *Hello!* magazine. I was pictured in the group centrefold, throwing confetti, with a staple through my nose.

***

Earlier on, I had complained to Christopher that I hadn't had a dip since my arrival in Barbados.

"Oh, for God's sake!" he said. "*Moan, moan, moan!* I'll take you to the beach in the morning."

He did. It was very early. The beautiful sea, a sort of azure bluey green, was most inviting. Only two other people were swimming. They turned out to be Jimmy Perry — writer of the comedy series *Dad's Army*, *Hi-Di-Hi* and others — and his companion Mary Husband, who was a BBC costume designer. They were as surprised as me for us to see each other. A somewhat surreal reunion.

"That's enough chatting!" shouted Christopher from the shore. "Time to get you back to your rehearsals!"

The Mikado was slotted in for more performances by Johnny Kidd.

We were having a wonderful time, except actor Stewart Permutt, who had to be flown back to the UK to dispose of some emotional baggage. Our wonderful time hiccuped again when Maris, the stage director, ran over a local lady driving her moke. It wasn't fatal but there was to be a court case. Biggins, Brad and I turned up at the magistrates' courts in Holetown to support her. We weren't let in because we were wearing shorts. But Johnny Kidd supported her and she was let off.

I wrote to Stuart in London constantly and was sorry that he couldn't join me in the idyll. He was busy as Head of Protocol back at Westminster Abbey. But I promised him I'd show him Barbados someday — and I did, years later, when he retired. We went on a world trip and stayed in the Discovery Bay Hotel in Barbados, where the ceiling fell in.

But Stuart thought it was the best place in the world.

I was the luckiest director to have been given the job in Barbados — thank you, Christopher!

We all hoped for another season the following year. I'd wanted to do *The Gondoliers* but that hope was scuppered by Luciano Pavarotti who said he'd like to do an operatic evening. A star-bedazzled Johnny Kidd agreed. So that was all of us off the radar.

An operatic evening by Pavarotti didn't come cheap. First, there was a huge orchestra for Puccini and Verdi, plus the star's entourage... and the big sword of Damocles — that Mr Pavarotti might not turn up. Operatic stars are notorious for cancelling; think back to Montserrat Caballé and *Vissi d'arte*! Signor Pavarotti insisted on TV coverage. His agent was in cahoots with his mistress. It would all cost Johnny Kidd a fortune.

We all assembled at Barbados airport for the return to the UK — Maris nervous, in case the Magistrates changed their minds about the incident with the local lady, still in hospital, and bundled Maris off the hoosegow.

Home we went.

Brad Fitt had become a best pal and still is. We never lost contact.

A birthday card for Biddy Baxter

Scene 18

She who must be obeyed

Biddy Baxter, in her post-*Blue Peter* days, was an assistant to the Director-Generals. She organised seminars. These were working conventions of the great and the good — who weren't yet at the top of their tree but might prove influential when the BBC Charter came up for renewal. At which time they would remember Biddy's lovely gatherings which were always followed by a fish pie lunch — and endorse the Corporation. These assemblies were of about 50 people. Biddy recruited people she knew from the staff to act as BBC hosts and hostesses to smallish groups of the delegates. I was one.

Somebody asked me, "What does a 'BBC host' mean?" I told them that if they'd give me a quid I'd dance with them! Being host to a group meant you were up for grabs to field questions the attendees were too reticent to ask at the seminar. I was looking after a bunch of politicians. Bernie Grant, the MP for Tottenham, nabbed me and harangued me about the

IS THAT YOU, MAUREEN?

lack of racial minorities in BBC programmes.

"We've got Moira Stewart reading the news," I placated.

"Hmmmm. Not enough."

I had to take the gang to the office of James Moir, the Head of Light Entertainment. He had pioneered *The Generation Game*. Mr Moir was on the phone in his office. Queenie, his secretary, told us to wait. She was old school, having inherited Mr Moir from Billy Cotton. We could overhear Mr Moir on his phone, making dates at the Groucho Club and other media Meccas. It was very impressive. We went into his palatial office.

"Jeremy! Great to see you!"

I'd never met Jimmy Moir.

I introduced the gaggle. Bernie Grant was still smouldering about the lack of BBC ethnic representation.

"Before I say anything, I'd like to show you the Golden Rose of Montreux trophies," Mr Moir declared, as he indicated the Rose d'Or pyramid. "These trophies have been won by the BBC over the decades. And the very first one was won by the *The Black and White Minstrel Show*."

Whoops.

At the fish pie lunch, Biddy asked me how I got on with my allocated seminar participants. I told her about the Golden Rose of Montreux trophies and Bernie Grant. Her eyes narrowed dangerously under the blue eye shadow.

James Moir swiftly became the Controller of BBC Radio 2, where he achieved huge success with Terry Wogan.

There was another seminar when we were instructed to engage Alasdair Milne, the Director-General, with questions which would detain him at the fish pie lunch. Little did he know, it was Julius Caesar time. His office was being emptied and the contents deposited in tea chests — Alasdair Milne was being removèd!

Biddy always issued a Brazilian rainforest of papers detailing the people you had to look after, plus the seminar's schedule. The thorough Biddy had everything written down:

> "Take the delegates to the Sixth Floor Suite. And at 11am, after outlines by the BBC omnipotents, take them to the Newsroom. Let them stand in front of the weather map — introduce them to Moira Stewart, hopefully. Then take them to the small service

lift to B209 (in the basement) where they'll meet the engineers engaged in Digital Television Development — (with luck they'll have a clip of Penelope Keith and Patricia Routledge — and not be wearing sandals and socks). Then return the guests to the Sixth Floor Suite."

Of course, you had to do a recce for the Seminar the day before.

"I'm off on a recce for tomorrow's seminar," I told Lesley, my PA.

Dutifully, I set off with Biddy's vast sheaf of papers. First stop on the agenda, the main lift at the TV Centre, which went up to the sixth floor. Good — all the seats were lined up. Then down the corridor to the newsroom. That was all sorted. And then down the corridor to the small service lift, in which I'd take the guests to B209. I pushed the button, the lift opened, I went in. The doors slid shut. I looked up. On each section, chiselled, with hate, into the panels was a derogatory, if not obscene, comment about our respected Director-General — today's genial host.

Oh dear.

This would not look good for the guests. Maybe I imagined it?

I arrived at the bottom of the lift ride. I went into B209.

"Hi, guys, pull out the stops for the DG's guests tomorrow," I said. "Sock it to them!"

An understatement. Digital TV development was unsockable.

I went back to the small service lift. The graffiti was still there. I hadn't imagined it! I went back to my office.

"Get me Biddy Baxter on the phone."

Lesley did.

"Hi, Biddy."

"Hello darling, everything OK?"

"I did a recce for the seminar."

"Oh darling, you didn't need to."

In Biddy language that meant, "Oh yes, you did have to."

"Well, yes, I did. There's a problem with the small service lift."

"Oh, I'll ring Head of Lifts. Is it sticking?"

"No sticking, Biddy, but there is some graffiti chiselled into the doors."

"What sort of graffiti?"

"Well, I really don't like to say."

"Tell me!" she barked.

"It's not very respectful. I don't like to tell you."

"*Tell-me-what-the-graffiti-says!*"

I told her.

A pause.

"Well, he *is!*" and slammed down the phone.

The next morning the small service lift looked like an NYPD murder scene, all taped off, and the main lifts of Television Centre were fiercely requisitioned for the guests of the seminar. All the staff were left to trudge up the stairs to their offices. I got the lift upstairs, smartly dressed, carrying all my files, and joined the bonhomie of the assembly.

Biddy, as ever, was the most wonderful hostess. At the end of the seminar, her tour de force flourish was to roll back the connecting doors of the Sixth Floor Suite and reveal the sumptuous fish pie lunch. Biddy was an eternal tour de force!

It was around this time that great rents appeared in the rich tapestry of my life. Vanya Kewley died, as did my parents. And Caroline Dawson. And Wendy Duggan and Ron Riches. And Ann Emery. And Dick Levin and his wife Paddy — Patricia Foy. And Monica Sims. The tapestry is now like frayed lace at my current age, resounding to heartfelt thuds as droppings off the perch constantly occur.

I'll put aside life's frailty for the mo — though it can never be put aside.

BETTIE'S GALLERY

Scene 19

Worth a lot when you're dead

I've always painted. Pictures, not walls. I always used to draw detailed storyboards for productions and now my favourite therapy is setting up the watercolours and paper with a picture in mind.

Bettie Morton MBE, a friend of Neil and Greg's, owned an art gallery in Brixton and she offered me an exhibition. Brixton is one of the more imaginative suburbs of South-East London, vibrant and colourful. Bettie's gallery was on Atlantic Road, off Coldharbour Lane. Bettie had invited me to a preceding exhibition, before my paintings were to be displayed, with other artists in her gallery.

Brixton was easy from Battersea, the 37 bus en route to Peckham — where I got my paintings framed. I sauntered down Coldharbour Lane, which had an awful lot of barber shops. At the last one, a rapscallion in a Rasta hat accosted me.

"Wanna buy some skank?"

"No, thank you" I replied primly — then curiously, "How much is it?"

"If you don't want to buy, then you don't want to know how much. I'm a philosopher. Whadda you doin' down here?"

"I'm on my way to an exhibition."

"I like art."

"Then look in. It's in a gallery round the corner."

Bettie's preview was pretty packed. Previews are great freeloading opportunities. Everyone looking at each other and not at the pictures. But it was a good preview. Bettie was a great hostess to everyone.

"We're looking forward to yours next week, Jeremy," she announced. "Jeremy has pictures here next week!"

The milieu gathered around the window of the gallery. Suddenly, they parted, as if Carabosse had come into the room.

Jammed up against the glass was the philosopher.

"Who's that?" asked Bettie.

"Oh, a local businessman I met en route. I'll ask him in."

I did. He was affable with the attendees. I had to go. I was meeting the blessed Stuart in merciful Mayfair for dinner. "I've asked loads to your exhibition," he told me. "They've never been to Brixton before."

The next day I went back to Bettie's to finalise my exhibition. She was in a mood when I arrived.

"What's the matter?"

"What's the matter? What's the *matter*? You invited a major drug pusher to my preview last night!"

"Sorry about that."

When I left, I ran into the philosopher in Coldharbour Lane.

"Did you enjoy the pictures last night?"

"They were OK but it was the best night's business I ever did!"

***

I shared my exhibition with other artists. Stuart invited some friends, who were petrified walking down the streets of Brixton. They were just innocently sinister — the streets, not Stuart's friends. A lovely preview. The philosopher did not turn up — flushed with his profits from the last time. My pictures were doing well, along with other sharing artists.

"Your pictures are doing well," said Bettie. "Go and say hello to that lady."

"Why?"

"She's just bought two."

I went to the lady.

"Thank you for buying those two pictures."

"They're just right for my hairdressing salon in Streatham.

"I'm sure Monet would have aspired to that."

"Money had nothing to do with it! A woman in one picture looks like my uncle, who was a drag queen in Dublin. Why are you talking to me?"

"I painted them."

"Well, they will be worth a lot when you're dead!"

Pondering on this macabre appraisal of my pictures, I went home and started to write a play, all thanks to the lady's comment.

It was about an art gallery that bumped off the older artists to boost the sale prices of their works. I called it *Sudden Deaths*. 'Death' in a title is always good box office in the home counties' theatres — I wasn't aspiring to Shaftesbury Avenue with my oeuvre!

Brenda Longman (the voice of Soo the panda in *Sooty* and a great pal) agreed for my play to have a reading in Farnham Theatre, which she was running. Farnham Rep Theatre in a marquee next to the bureaucratically closed Redgrave Theatre. She assembled a great cast and enlisted Maurice Thorogood to direct. Maurice had been in *Grandad* for me with Clive

Dunn. Ann Emery was to be in the reading, playing an elderly soon-to-be-bumped-off lesbian sculptress. Elizabeth Counsell was the lead.

The Saturday afternoon performance of *Sudden Deaths* went well in the tent, with the seated actors reading on stage. Stuart brought a lot of his Livery — the Worshipful Company of Gold and Silver Wyre Drawers — and other friends, all motored down to Farnham.

Neil Hardie caught my eye after a laugh for one exchange of dialogue. "How dreadful! Dead! How did Gina, the cleaner, react when she discovered the body?"

"She was devasted. She had another cleaning job at midday."

The eye-catch was a mischievous glint at the thought of Mary, our mutual cleaner. Mary would have had that sort of priority.

After the reading, Ann Emery went off to spend the rest of the weekend with her friend Charles Vance and his wife, the Lady Imogen, in Kent. Charles was a distinguished theatrical producer who was having a summer season in Sidmouth, Devon. He asked Ann why she was coming to see them from Farnham.

"I was in a play reading."

"A play?"

"By Jeremy Swan."

"I know him. Was the play any good?"

"Have a read. I've still got my script in my bag."

On the Monday, she left the Vances to read the script. Charles rang me within the week.

"The Lady Imogen and I read your play. We'd like to do it in the Sidmouth Season."

"That's great, Charles. Big thanks. I'll get my agent to call you."

Sara Randall, my agent, had been at the Farnham show. I phoned her.

"Wonderful, darling. I'll ring Charles and discuss a fee."

Charles Vance didn't like fee discussions. What producer does?

"A fee, Sara! A *fee*! Jeremy wants a *fee*? I'm featuring his play in a prestigious play festival and *he wants a fee*? I'm putting his name, up there with Agatha Christie, Alan Ayckbourn, Neil Simon, Aldous Huxley, and Francis Durbridge and *he wants a fee*?"

That put a stop to the fee discussion. If pushed any further, there'd be no play by Jeremy Swan in the Sidmouth Season!

The director, Pat Brackenbury, came to lunch at my house and I read her the play. I could see that *Sudden Deaths* was in her very capable hands.

I took a trip to Sidmouth to see another play in Charles' repertoire.

A question, reader: What's the worst thing that can happen in Neil Simon's *Plaza Suite*, a play about a hotel room? Answer: The door handle falls off!

A lot of Black-&-Deckering was heard during the interval.

The company was very good. Their weekly rep was a hard grind. A play was performed Thursday, Friday and on Saturday as a matinee and during the evening. Then again on the following Monday, Tuesday and Wednesday. You could see three plays on a fortnight's holiday in Sidmouth.

All my friends and family were very enthusiastic and excited about my play opening, so I booked rooms in the Bedford Hotel, where I stayed to see *Plaza Suite*.

The day after the American play, I visited the set designer, Robert Sherwood, busy churning out weekly scenery. "It's very nice of you to call in to see me, Jeremy. There was never a sign of Agatha Christie, Alan Ayckbourn, Neil Simon, Aldous Huxley nor Francis Durbridge!"

I arrived back in Sidmouth ahead of the first night. I wanted to see the dress rehearsal. "Don't!" warned Poppy Corbett, Charles' producer. "It throws them!"

Well, that's understandable. They didn't want me kerfuffling about.

The Manor Pavilion Theatre had a big bar at the back. I booked a catering company for a supper party for after the first night, plus an open-tab bar. The party was mainly for the actors. Actors are always starving.

I sat with Stuart for the first night. My family had flown into Exeter (the nearest airport) from Dublin. Anna, Peter and Robina (Stuart's brother and his wife), Deborah MacMillan (widow of Sir Kenneth MacMillan of the Royal Ballet), Hannah Gordon and her husband Robert, Tony Trowles (librarian of Westminster Abbey), Elizabeth Ferguson (also of the Royal Ballet) and my agent Sara Randall trailed down from London.

Pat Brackenbury did a great job. She had the play open with extras examining the painting exhibition. Then, to Saint-Saëns' *Danse Macabre*, she had the main cast sashay through the audience, onto the stage and the scenes began.

A good interval buzz — always welcome — and, at the end there was the party, which was pretty lively. The local paper's write-up described the play as "Unusual, enjoyable and entertaining."

It could have been a description of the audience.

£60 owing. My Tom Merryfield sculpture

Scene 20
Tom and Blackie

This one is a beloved digression — Blackie and Tom Merrifield. They were in my life for nigh on 50 years.

For one special week of *Jackanory* shows, I replaced the usual punctuating illustrations with *tableau vivant*, using inserts with dancers. The *tableau* came from traditional stories, narrated by Bernard Cribbins, including *The Emperor's New Clothes*. The *vivant* was students from the Ballet Rambert dance company. I needed one strong professional male dancer, so I rang choreographer Jo Cook. She immediately suggested Tommy Merrifield. Unusually, he answered the phone when I called — I was later told he was never allowed to — and we made a date for him to come to my office so I could have a look at him.

In he came. He looked fine, an attractive little pixie-like Australian guy with a shy demeanour — I quickly discovered that he was a very good actor! The rehearsals were fun as I pretended to be a choreographer, with a lot of hand waving and pointy step routines. Anna Home looked on as the executive producer.

Tommy Merrifield was a great cast addition and got on famously with the Rambert students. And he took my directions with enthusiasm.

"Tommy, in *Beauty and the Beast* you're playing Beauty's father, not her grandfather!"

After the final rehearsal he came to me and shyly said, "Jeremy, I'd like to offer you an invitation!"

"What kind of invitation?"

"I'd like you to come to a party with Blackie and me!"

I thought quickly; Blackie must be his exotic boyfriend or his dog.

"I'd love to, Tommy."

"Good, it will be at our place in Elm Row, Hampstead. Next week? I've told Blackie all about you."

The five *Jackanory* episodes were soon recorded. Tommy knew Bernard Cribbins from some West End show they'd been in, which added to the conviviality. Anna had warmed to her role as our own Ninette de Valois and we were delighted with the finished result. It paved the way for *Jackanory Playhouse*, a series of fully-staged plays with real live actors.

The Elm Row date arrived. I took the Underground to Hampstead, after telling Neil Hardie and Michael Marks, with whom I lived in Clapham, "If I'm not home by midnight, ring the police!"

No 1 Elm Row had big wooden gates. I went through, clutching a bunch of blooms, and saw a tall house with a circular pond in the front garden. The door was opened by an elderly lady.

"I'm May. They are expecting you upstairs in the drawing room, Jeremy."

Up I went to a long-pillared room which was filled with a lively crowd. A lady with long flowing blonde hair greeted me warmly.

"Jeremy, we are so glad you could come. I'm Blackie, Tommy's wife."

So much for imagining exotic boyfriends and dogs!

It was a wonderful party — Blackie and Tommy were amazing hosts — and it was the first of many great parties that I was invited to at Elm Row. They were glittering evenings. Blackie was an artistic entrepreneur. Her main occupation was supplying all the artwork for the guest bedrooms and environs of the Trust House Forte Hotels. She had a vast stable of artists and Tommy was wildly artistic. As time went on, he became a painter of renown, encouraged by Blackie. There was an exhibition of his works at the White Elephant on the River, a restaurant owned by Blackie's friend Stella Richman, who was a boss at London Weekend Television.

Blackie almost framed the rags with which Tommy wiped his oil painting brushes! His work sold and Blackie sold pictures from the artists in her stable. I bought one for my friend Neil Hardie — a vivid green print of a cow under a tree by Bernard Cheeseman.

On one visit to Elm Row, I saw on the table a fabulous bronze sculpture of Terry Gilbert, the dancer — arms spread, a leg lifted. I was transfixed. What a statue! Tom had moved from painting to sculpture. This was one of his first.

"Buy it!" said Blackie. "You can have it on easy terms."

"Oh Blackie, I can't! I've just bought a house in Clapham. I'm saving up to buy a fridge."

"Jeremy! It's December! You don't need a fridge!"

So, I bought it. On easy terms. In the base of the statue, currently sitting on my mantel shelf, there's an inserted note from their housekeeper May: "You still owe £60!"

I paid eventually — and I also bought a fridge.

On my mantelpiece, there are four Tom Merrifield bronzes, with a lot of his pictures around the house. I recently donated a huge nude picture of Jay Jolley by Tom to the Royal Academy of Dance.

***

Blackie and Tom — he was now Tom rather than Tommy — also held legendary 'white' parties. White clothes, not complexions. At one, I stood on a balcony in Elm Row with choreographer and dance teacher Biddy Espinosa, looking at the swirling white-attired guests in the garden below, massing around the circular pond. "It looks like something from *One Flew Over the Cuckoo's Nest!*" she said.

Tom and Blackie went on to have huge sculpture exhibitions in London's Royal Festival Hall. I was recruited as an attendant. Many women fell madly in love with Tom — and were very quickly put aside by Blackie.

My friend Caroline Dawson said to me one day, "We never hear from Sally Bulloch." Sally was an actress, who used to give great PR parties in London. "I hear she's gone to live with a sculptor in Hampstead."

I didn't know many sculptors in Hampstead — but I knew one!

Another party followed in Elm Row with Blackie, as ever, the great hostess. She called out. "Sally, can you bring in the canapés?"

Sally Bulloch appeared in an apron with a tray.

"Hello, Jeremy. Have a canapé!"

"Hi Sally!" — I did. "Wonderful to see you!"

"I don't believe it!" exclaimed Caroline.

It didn't take Poirot to work out that Blackie had a canny machination underway. The best way to prevent shenanigans behind the bike shed was to bring the *shenaniger* into the fold. Sally was now a waitress, supervised by the indomitable May.

Blackie and Tom sometimes used to visit the Forest Mere Health Spa to charge up their batteries. One day, a dishevelled woman emerged from the steam room as Blackie was about to go in. "Don't go in! There's a sex maniac on the loose in there!"

"Oh, that's probably my husband," exclaimed Blackie.

***

The Merrifields were always up for grabs. Unintentionally, of course. Two rapscallions poached away their Royal Festival Hall venue with an exhibition by American painter Robert Heindel.

Blackie was philosophical — the grabbers were bastards.

Blackie's sister was Joan Rhodes, a strongwoman who tore telephone books in half and once spectacularly lifted Bob Hope on her head at the London Palladium! Joan told me she used to bake the phone books in the oven to make them tearably brittle. She didn't like Tom and he wisely kept his distance from his Amazonian sister-in-law. Joan's picture, painted by Dame Laura Knight, still hangs in the Royal Academy.

Blackie and Tom are interred in the grounds of the Christ Church in Hampstead. I'm constantly reminded of them, with all his pictures and statues around my house. I love them dearly — Tom and Blackie, and the pictures.

Well, that was a bit sad. I'd better cheer things up...

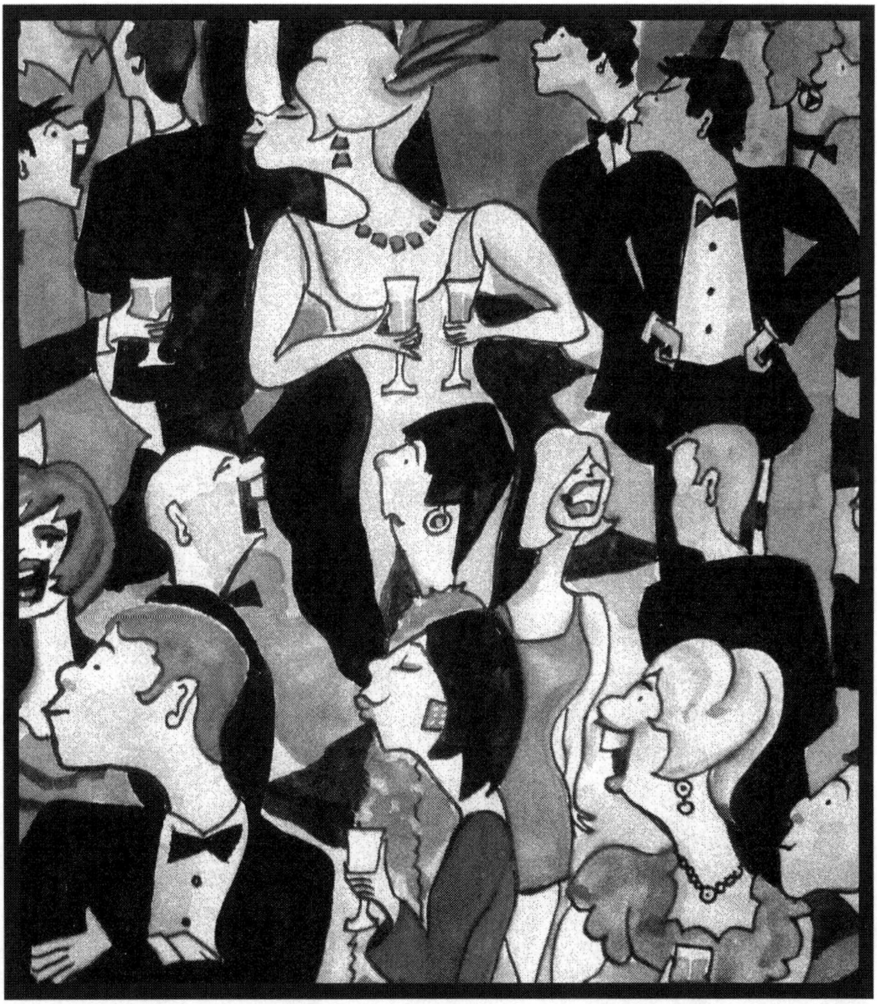

Stuart at the prow

Scene 21

Cruising

Anna Home was invited on a cruise by Chris Gidney, who had been my AFM on the *Blue Peter* pantos and was now a theme producer for cruise lines. His latest cruise was themed around the 'Legends of Children's Television'. Anna said she'd rather scale the Eiger, but she recommended Jeremy Swan, who she had heard give a rollicking speech at a livery dinner hosted by Stuart.

"Great!" said Chris Gidney. "I'll call him!"

Stuart and I had already done a cruise — "two for the price of one" up the Amazon. We had an elderly passenger ensemble — five died at sea. The ship was the *Marco Polo*. I called it the 'Marco Polio' because of the preponderance of crutches wielded by most of the passengers. The Amazon? We should have been going to Lourdes!

Nonetheless, our six-week trip crossed the Atlantic to South America. Olga, the mistress of the Captain, and I stood at the entrance of the Amazon — she was in charge of excursions, and he was in charge of the ship. We marvelled at the sea becoming golden with silt flowing out of the estuary of the great waterway. The Amazon was so vast that we couldn't see the shores.

"Just a minute," I hear you cry. "Five died!"

Dying is an occupational hazard in cruising. Considering the average age, there are always a number of passengers in the Grim Reaper's sights. Also, if you're still fit, though ancient, it's cheaper to cruise than to go into the local Setting Sun Rest Home. Many octogenarians stay afloat all year round. These canny old codgers and crones astutely study cruises online, and then pounce when the cruise line is practically paying them to come on board.

Onto the deaths. One woman fell over a tombstone on Devil's Island — a few others drifted off. One 95-year-old gent was left waiting on a jetty in a wheelchair in 110 degrees of blazing Brazilian sun, flanked by the tropics. He was waiting to go on a piranha fishing trip with his wife. A local Brazilian, who looked like one of the Three Stooges in a grass skirt, didn't fancy a 95-year-old in a wheelchair in his bark canoe, so he paddled away into the reeds. The tender of the ship took the old man back to the *Marco Polo* eventually, but he came over queer in the cabin and passed away from jungle exposure in Manaus General Hospital.

His wife came into the bar at Happy Hour. I rushed to sympathise, while other passengers looked away in embarrassment and nose-dived into their Manhattans.

"I'm so sorry," I said and embraced the just-widowed lady.

"He was alright when we were going piranha fishing this morning," she declared,

"You should put that on his headstone," I replied.

"Where are all the bodies going?" I nervously asked Stuart later.

"I don't know but the pastry chef is looking a bit frazzled."

* * *

We sat every night at a table for eight, with six extremely amiable people. Naturally, the conversation veered in the Agatha Christie direction.

"Haven't seen the woman with the purple hair and the big diamond for a few days. She's been staggering a bit!"

"Hmmmmm!" But mainly we were roaring with laughter.

There were various stops before our ultimate Amazon destination, Manaus. The *Marco Polo* was able to navigate the voyage because she had a flat bottom. Big-bottomed ships don't. One stop, themed 'Boi Bumba', sounded promising — but was a rehearsal for a local village's participation in the Rio de Janeiro Carnival.

The villagers welcomed us — as much as an Amazon village can welcome 800 deck-maniacal Brits. Local drinks were being whizzed around and everyone was guzzling them back. It was caipirinha, a lethal, local hooch. I snatched Stuart's from his hand.

"Oh, this is delicious. A delicate flavour with a hint of—"

"No, it's not, Stuart! Have a beer!"

The passengers were now as mad as rats on Brazilian booze! The village gymnasium hadn't quite got the atmosphere of the vibrant streets of Rio, awash with drag queens but, nevertheless, with lurid lighting, great drumming, and gallons more caipirinhas ("Have another beer, Stuart!"), the gym became Rio. Loads of locals, feathers inserted into every orifice, thundered onto the stage. It was terrific, with tom-toms beating out huge routines.

The cruise audience was aflame with enthusiasm — some more inflamed than others. The spectacle ended with a climatic finale. Everyone rose to their feet, many filming the show on their devices and phones.

One man near the stage asked the guy in front if he enjoyed the show.

"What's it to do with you whether I did or not?" retorted the guy in front, somewhat belligerently, holding his large laptop aloft.

"It's to do with the fact that we hardly saw it, with you standing up with that bloody screen all through the show!" replied the other, taking a swing at him.

Fisticuffs and yelling ensued, swiftly curtailed by heavies from the ship barging into the fray. The first swinger was dragged off and imprisoned in his cabin, with his wife, for a week. The *Marco Polo* took a poor view of pugnacious passengers — and others, who didn't comply.

A couple were left on the quayside in Bequia. The husband had groped some female Russian dancers on stage during a ship's floor show. Olga and I looked down at the abandoned pair, shaking their fists in anguish at the departing ship.

"How are they going to get back?" I asked her.

Superciliously, Olga glanced at them. "Possibly, they'll pick up a ship to Barbados. And, possibly, get a plane to the UK and, possibly, go and collect their luggage in Tilbury."

This seemed rather cruel, I thought. Barbados was hundreds of miles away. Ships going there were infrequent and it would be a nightmare to get on an unbooked UK flight once in Barbados. The *Marco Polo*'s treatment of miscreants was unforgiving. Another couple were offloaded in St Lucia for some skullduggery with a credit card.

Manaus, our ultimate destination, was dominated by the spectacle of its magnificent opera house — a cultural centre when the Brazilian rubber plantations were at their peak; the plantations eventually moved to Malaysia, which was a severe blow to Brazil's industry. I was told that each seat in the opera house cost the lives of one hundred slaves. So did Rome's Colosseum, I suppose.

Onwards! There was a cruise where I replaced Anna — 'Legends of Children's Television'. The legends were Floella Benjamin, Melvyn Hayes Mick Robertson from ITV's *Magpie*, Valerie Singleton from *Blue Peter* and me, plus two chaps who had reinvented Gerry Anderson's *Thunderbirds*. We were to go to Madeira and the Canary Islands. These cruises were the most marvellous doddle. All you had to do was give one talk, usually in the morning, for 35 minutes — that's how long the audience's bladders could endure.

The Cruise Maritime, via Chris Gidney, the producer, gave you a smart outside cabin so you could see the sea, all meals, 50 percent off drinks, a laundry discount and a cheap rate for the ship's excursions. You could bring a friend or partner. "No, thank you," said Stuart. "I'm dubbing!" He didn't know what that meant, but he had heard me say it over the years when I had to pull out of his events.

The guests could either do stand-up or be interviewed by Chris Gidney. I opted for stand-up. Whenever a cruise schedule lists 'at sea' it meant that it was when the passengers had to be entertained on board — no excursion distraction. And that's when the likes of us were featured. We all went loyally to each other's performances. I sat with Melvyn Hayes while Floella was being interviewed, splendidly, by Chris Gidney. She told of her arrival in England via the Windrush generation and her early days in *Play School* and *Play Away*, in which I'd directed her. She concluded her session with the promise to hug all the audience members as they left the auditorium.

"Crikey! We'll be here all day," muttered Melvyn.

And then she burst into song. "*Smile! Though your heart is aching...*"

"Jesus," murmured Melvyn. "Have you got a song, Jeremy?"

I hadn't. He didn't. Floella had, and she was a triumph. She whipped the passengers into a near-Messianic frenzy, terminating with her heartfelt song.

Val Singleton told the story of the *Blue Peter* elephant shitting in the *Blue Peter* Studio. I was always sympathetic to that story. The poor elephant keeper never lived down his baby elephant's behaviour, even though the episode delighted millions.

Food is the main pastime on cruises — the passengers ate like starved animals. At 6.30 there was breakfast in the restaurants. The passengers were in a competition — "Who can eat the most?" Plates were piled with eggs, beans, bacon, potato cakes, waffles — edifices awaiting consumption. And at 10am there was hard-boiled-egg-stealing time, in case anyone was feeling peckish. At 11am it was coffee time with cakes and other assuagements. Then there was lunch — five courses of grills and more. But, panic not! There was then afternoon tea with Battenburg cakes and scones smothered in cream and jam.

Happy Hour then slid into the schedule. A couple of gins before quickly getting ready for dinner — all eight courses!

The first dinner sitting was at 6pm. We, the turns, sat at them, in tables screened off by Chris and his wife Katherine. The first sitting coincided with the ship's show — where half the audience went, before catching the second dinner sitting. We went to the repeat performance. The shows were wonderful. The young dancers worked their socks off. The evening ended with us all sitting in the bar, talking to the passengers who had paid to be entertained by us. Any slight tummy rumblings? No worries. Waiters appeared with platters of fried calamari and chicken legs — all scoffed down.

I was asked on another cruise. The theme, 'Cookery'.

"I know nothing about cookery," I said to Chris.

"Shut up, Jeremy! You can talk about anything."

At last, I persuaded Stuart to come with me.

The cast was the wonderful Rustie Lee, Jilly Goolden, the wine expert, Monisha Bharadwaj (big in curries), Chris Marlowe (who won *Come Dine with Me*) and Julia Behrens, a very nice girl who whipped up herbs.

And me.

I opened my spiel with, "You all remember Fanny Cradock?"

"Ah, yes!"

"She was on a show where she demonstrated cakes and confectionaries. Her husband, Johnny, had the last word in her programme: 'I sincerely hope that all your doughnuts turn out looking just like Fanny's.'"

Stuart was a great cruise companion. Everyone loved him, especially the gorgeous Rustie Lee. The thing about cruises is that, as entertainers,

Rustie Lee dishes up the cake!

you are up for grabs. A lot of the passengers are lovely, you make good friends. But there are semi-stalkers. One was Melvyn (not Hayes). He used to join us at our drinks. He was a taxi driver from Manchester. I quite liked him. He seemed to know everybody.

"Diane-Louise Jordan sends you her love, Jeremy — and John Leslie."

"Give them my love, Melvyn."

I was walking Rustie back to her cabin. "How does that fellow know all these people that I know?"

Rustie replied, philosophically, "He knows them like he knows us."

***

Chris Gidney called me. "I'm doing another cruise with *The Platinum Jubilee of The Queen*."

"Terrific — I've got lots of Queen stories!"

"Actually, Jeremy, we don't want you. It's the lovely chap you brought on the last cruise. We want him — Stuart Holmes."

"What about me? I've got great stories about old queens."

"Save them for the boiler room, Jeremy. I want Stuart."

It had turned into *All About Eve*!

Stuart was delighted. Derek Deane was sending me texts addressed to Margo Channing, signed Addison DeWitt — as played by Bette Davis and George Sanders in Joseph L. Mankiewicz's movie.

Stuart was to talk about his time as Head of Protocol at Westminster Abbey and the times he had worked on huge parties for Lady Elizabeth Anson, the Queen's cousin. He was a sure-fire win — and he was able to take me on the cruise. His co-stars were Dickie Arbiter and Katie Nicholl, both royal journalists, Andrew Lloyd Webber's archivist Mark Fox and royal historical novelist Nicola Tallis.

Stuart's interview with Chris was a triumph.

The only look-in I got was to read out the lesson at the Reverend Cindy Kent's service on a Sunday. Cindy was the cruise vicarette. She had married Chris and Katherine. The Reverend managed to give everyone covid.

Chris, placatable, booked me on another cruise — this time to Norway, with actress April Walker, Floella and her husband Keith, Jan Leeming and John Sergeant.

While in Bergen, John Sergeant and I visited the historic home of Edvard Grieg, Norway's most famous classical composer. It looked like the Bates Motel. Workmen were loading crates onto trucks when we arrived.

"Oh drat," said John. "We're too late! The Griegs are moving out!"

For my talk, I told the old stories about the pantos I did on the BBC 40 years ago, with the Genies of the Ring and the Lamp played by Floella Benjamin and Christopher Biggins. I reminded the audience that Biggins would be doing panto in Darlington the following Christmas and that Floella continued in her role as the Right Honourable Baroness Benjamin of Beckenham in the House of Lords.

When you get a good part you keep on playing it.

***

Hold it! Hold it! A major digression looms. Stuart Manning, my esteemed publisher, has had the temerity to suggest that my narrative should have more 'grit'. Deep-felt emotion, heartbreak, unshed tears…

OK. That's there, Stuart. Dear ones passed away; parents, pals and quite a big cast. I don't want to drag readers down that morbid motorway.

"Weren't you fired from *Doctor Who*?" Stuart asks, morbidly.

That's pretty morbid to him. He's a huge *Doctor Who* fan.

Decades ago, I was working as an assistant floor manager duty stand-by in the BBC Studio Management office. Duty stand-by meant that you clocked in if somebody else didn't clock in. The *Doctor Who* AFM hadn't. He was off sick. The on-duty supervisor announced, "You've got to go to Studio 1, Jeremy, and stand in for the AFM on *Doctor Who*."

"Great, I love Ian Fleming!"

"No, Jeremy. Not *Dr. No*, *Doctor Who!*"

I went down to Studio 1. *Doctor Who* was in full flow at the start of their recording day. The place was ablaze with frantic activity — huge sci-fi sets, loads of actors dressed up as monsters and other horrors, Daleks being trundled around. No sign of a Doctor.

The main job of the AFM was dealing with props. They were all kept in huge green cages. I had to distribute these to the key players.

"I'm only the stand-by AFM," I entreated the actors. "Could you help me, and identify your required props?"

They did. They were mainly very sweet. One wasn't. A major shit — he'll be grateful that I never knew his name. He was dressed up as a kind of astronaut. He was going on and on about his 'sting-ray gun'. I didn't know what a sting-ray gun looked like from a pea-shooter.

"I'll get your sting-ray gun as soon as I can. There's an awful lot of guns, sting-rays and otherwise, in this prop cage. Please be patient."

He wasn't.

They were recording. Mr Kind-of-an-astronaut was stood looking at some plonker dressed as a frog. Mr Kind-of-an-astronaut kept forgetting his lines.

The production assistant stopped the recording. The director upstairs was going mad through the earphones. "Why can't the motherfucker say his lines?" he yelled.

Maybe he didn't say motherfucker — BBC directors were very polite in those days — but that's what he meant.

The PA, ever a pacifier twixt director and actors, asked calmly, "Trouble with the dialogue? Let's have another go. Shall we? Another go?"

"*Trouble with the dialogue?*" snarled Mr Kind-of-an-astronaut. "I'll tell you the trouble with the dialogue! That bloody temp of an AFM won't give me my sting-ray gun!"

All eyes swivelled to the bloody temp of an AFM standing beside the prop cage. Grit struck — and deep-felt emotion.

I hollered out, "Get your own fucking sting-ray gun, Mary!"

A monster design for Monster TV, *complete with comedy flounce*

Scene 22
Finish up

Jim Eldridge had written *Monster TV* for BBC Children's Programmes — the title as on the tin. This time, our roles were reversed; along with directing, Jim suggested that I co-write with him. Elaine Sperber, executive producer of Children's — ex-Disney — shouted down a corridor to me one day.

"Jeremy! I've just watched a repeat of *Julia Jekyll and Harriet Hyde*."

"That's very sweet of you, Elaine."

"It's not sweet at all! It's word-for-word episode four of *Monster TV*!"

"Elaine, the audience *adores* repetition."

Soon after, having finally accepted redundancy from the BBC — and their attractive pension — I was launched back into the world as a freelance TV director. Ed Pugh, Head of ITV Children's Programmes in Manchester, rang me up.

"How would you like to direct *Sooty*?"

This was on the strength of my directing *Fraggle Rock* and *The Secret Lives of Toys*. I was big in puppet circles.

Glove puppet Sooty was a TV legend. He'd been going for decades, with Sweep and Soo. I felt an *éminence grise* at being appointed his TV director! I went to see the producers, John Stephens and his wife, Helen. They lived in a lovely house in Twickenham — known as the House that Sooty Built.

"You must know the Dykes who live further down," said John.

"Ruby and Jocasta?"

"No, Jeremy! Greg Dyke and his family."

The series was filmed in the good ol' Granada Studios in Manchester's Quay Street, next to *Coronation Street*. This was before the whole shebang moved to Salford.

John inveigled *Coronation Street*'s stars to appear in *Sooty*. Liz Dawn, otherwise known as Vera Duckworth, did a scene with Soo the Panda in the make-up room. "Oh, Soo! It's wonderful to be, at last, working with a real star!"

Soo was voiced by Brenda Longman, who has become a great friend. She instigated my play in Farnham. Stuart, years later, instigated a show with Brenda for the Gold and Silver Wyre Drawers Livery Company in Leighton House. It was a sort of revue, with Colin Sell playing the piano, and me. Brenda recruited Rosemary Ashe of *The Phantom of the Opera* and *Les Misérables* fame to help out. It soon turned into The Rosie Ashe Show and was very enthusiastically received. The main performers got a load of dosh. I got a pot of herbs; one Liveryman of the Gold and Silver Wyre Drawers, John Walsham, owned a garden centre.

In the *Sooty* show, Sooty's pal, Sweep was squeaked by Brian Sandford — a puppeteer so dedicated to his role that he spoke in squeaks all the time, with Sweep's reed in his mouth. Sooty whispered his demands into Richard Cadell's ear, who translated them to the viewer.

"Izzy wizzy! Let's get busy!" and Sooty would wave his little wand.

It was a very busy shoot. I was somewhat traumatised when I saw twenty grubby Sootys swishing around in the washing machine.

A rather alarming scenario occurred.

"Wouldn't it be wonderful if Sweep could walk!" declared some deranged crew member. There were obvious preventions. Sweep had no legs. "But if he had..." persisted the mad innovator.

I kept well out of the mobility miracle.

Yet the miracle was achieved. A pair of stumpy back paws would be attached to a cup-like structure and the walking about would be achieved by remote control on a joystick. The body of Sweep — stuffed and rigid

— would be shoved in the cup, and *voilà*, there was the legged Sweep!

Moon-landing fervour gripped the inventors, wrestling to control the joystick. The initial walk-about was to be filmed in the local Manchester Park, curiously observed by dog walkers and their charges. A flat surface was found on a nearby path — necessarily flat as the legs could not manoeuvre uneven terrain. Sweep was standing. The camera rolled. The remote control glowed.

"Action!" I said to the remote controller.

Sweep set off on a staggering progression. He had no tail but that did not matter. The weird automaton stomped along. The on-looking real dogs howled and fled as far away as possible. Their owners reacted in terror, as if observing an alien who had just landed. They'd never seen anything so terrifying, confirmed by their dogs yowling in panic behind the bushes. The horror of the walking Sweep was an anathema.

"No more legs!" was the ultimatum from John Stephens, the producer.

Legless, we made the series.

I was booked to do another. This time back in the old *Fraggle Rock* studios in Maidstone. *Sooty* was getting very powerful with Richard Cadell, who had bought the *Sooty* franchise. Then Richard booked me for yet another series

I was getting a bit Sooty-ed out.

My last *Sooty* was on location in Brean, in Somerset — at a funfair, owned by Richard's brother, David. Richard put us all up in mobile homes. Those creepy-looking residences are dotted along coastal areas, throughout the country. I wasn't made to live in a mobile home. It was alright for a gypsy whittling pegs, but not for me.

Richard lived in a splendid Malibu-type house further up the coast, with cow-size statues of cows grazing in the grounds. He had wonderful aspirations as to how the series should look; some extremely ambitious — and often extremely difficult to achieve. After directing twelve episodes, enough was enough — the immobility of the mobile home was doing my 'ead in! That and driving miles back to London every weekend.

I went to Sue Kendall, the production manager, with my exit intentions and she came up with a clever strategy which she would put to Richard. Before I started the shoot, a fellow freelance director Adrian Hedley rang me to wish me well. This was setting the trap which would enable me to escape Sooty's clutches.

Sue calmly said to Richard, "Jeremy is going to have to edit his twelve episodes. So, it's best he gets going on that — and we bring in Adrian."

Richard went a bit ape-shit. But I stood firm.

And so did Sue. Soon, I was installed in a comfortable editing suite with a very comfortable editor in Soho's D'Arblay Street. There were lots of video houses established in the area. The older facilities had long since moved out, though some elderly hostesses could be seen taking mass at St Patrick's in Soho Square, where my Mikado, Stefan Bednarczyk, played the organ.

Anyway, sliding smoothly away from *Sooty*...

* * *

I love London — and Dublin too — but London claimed me more, from the time I went to stay in The Vale, Acton, seventy years ago, when I arrived, by boat and train, to audition for the Old Vic.

A great introduction to the brutality of 'that's showbusiness!' — I didn't get the audition.

There was a time long before that, when Dad brought me to see his country's capital when I was eight. We stayed with my Uncle Niall and Auntie Kay in their flat in Sydenham, next to Crystal Palace. Hillcrest Road is long gone. All around there is developed with flats and new houses. London is a city of continual architectural change. The skyline from Waterloo Bridge is the spectacle of a magnificent metropolis.

You rightly assume that this is a major digression.

And then there are the restaurants. London abounds with them. As a *bon viveur*, I have always eaten out. There's always someone who will cook you lunch or dinner — or even breakfast — in a nearby greasy spoon. If you don't want to cook, why should you?

In the sixties, there was the Wimpy Café in Kensington Church Street where the egg Wimpy was a gourmet delight. Opposite, if you wanted to spend more on your supper, was La Barca. Up the road was The Ark at Notting Hill Gate. They always came up trumps!

Michael Staniforth, my *Rentaghost* star, while in *A Chorus Line* at Drury Lane, took me to a new restaurant in Covent Garden. It was all the rage. Biggins was always there. That *made* it the rage. The restaurant was called Joe Allen. All of showbiz was there nearly every night. We'd leave at

FINISH UP

IAM! Christopher told me that his bank manager suspected he was being blackmailed by a 'Joe Allen'. You could only pay bills by cheque then — no swiping or carding!

There were other eateries. Round the corner was Luigi's on Tavistock Street. And further over in Soho, there was Bianchi's, managed by Elena Salvoni. Bianchi's was where Marconi invented radio. I was introduced to it by Michael Campbell who was the best friend of Shelah Richards in Dublin. "I've come here because it's calm!" he shouted as he banged his hand on the table, which broke all the wine glasses.

Elena was forgiving because she loved him. I was frightened!

Opposite Bianchi's in Frith Street was the L'Osteria Lariana. Kenneth Williams took me there: "It's fabulous. Fab grub — and hardly anyone ever comes in there!"

Giovanni was the owner, and he had a dubious chef — whom Kenneth loved and was the reason why it was always nearly empty — who sat there puffing away on his Silk Cut and swigging on a gin and tonic. Next door was Ronnie Scott's and then La Belle Etoile, which Elena Salvoni took over. The Etoile was a bit expensive, but she gave us cheap rates. Later, she moved up Charlotte Street to open a reincarnation of the Etoile where she reigned supreme. But I still remember her husband, Aldo, totting up the bills at his desk in Bianchi's: "I'm charging more for all the *pane!*"

Opposite the Etoile in Frith Street was Gerry's Club, which was an actors' go-to. Gerry Campion had played Billy Bunter in the TV series. I suppose 'seedy' might be the choice adjective for Gerry's. Way out in the sticks was the Queen's Elm in Fulham Road, where all the Irish actors convened. I went there once and it was so crowded with Irish actors that I fainted. The Salisbury pub in St Martin's Lane served great poached salmon sandwiches in the front bar. I used to go to Mama Malone's café in Golden Square with the theatrical agent Barry Burnett, where we'd do casting of his clients.

In Dublin, during the sixties, there was the Golden Orient, run by Mohammed 'Mike' Butt, the Pakistani Ambassador to Dublin. Next door was Gaj's, a Polish restaurant. You could eat very reasonably in these establishments. Further up the scale were Jammet's and the Trocadero. Opposite the Gate Theatre was the Gate Café, where my brother Nigel and I and the other kids in *Liffey Lane* would gorge in between shows on Saturdays, leaving a small dent in our weekly salaries of half a guinea —

That's 10/6d to your granny's money and 52 pence in today's. I managed to get the princely sum of £1 a week when I was in *The Seven Year Itch*.

Further down from the Gate in O'Connell Street, was Caffola's and their knickerbocker glories — the risqué title invited huge consumption. Bewley's had cafés on D'Olier Street and Grafton Street. Potato cakes and coffee were big on the menu. Elderly informed waitresses served. Instead of, "Ready to order, sir?" these ladies would ask, "Are you getting' it?" and reach for their pad, dangling on a long string tied around their waists.

Stuart had good joints around his area in Pimlico, which you can inhale as you walk along the Cubitt terraces. There's O'Sole Mio on Belgrave Road — *molto Italiano* with its staff Carlos, Simone and Maria. Round the corner there's the historic Grumbles Bistro. The manager there is Lincoln, a *Rentaghost* fan, who I was calling 'Washington', 'Kennedy' and 'Roosevelt' till Stuart severely corrected me. Down the road, there's the Seafresh — still fresh since I went there with Neil, Rosemary and Jillian in the seventies. And we go to an Oriental place in Wilton Street called the Dim T where Stuart always has exploded duck and pancakes and I eat nasi goreng, a fried rice dish, in happy memory of Kuala Lumpur.

Back in the day, location filming was enhanced by the delight of the catering wagon, starting with huge bacon sandwiches at dawn. All the studios had staff canteens — no Pret a Manger wraps, nor a paper-cup latte at the desk in those days.

Kenneth Williams and I were the first to arrive at a deserted BBC canteen in Lime Grove one time when we were filming a *Jackanory*. We perused the chalk-written menu.

"I'll have a curry," mused Kenneth.

"So will I."

A crone appeared behind the counter.

"We'll have two curries, please."

She dashed to the dumb waiter and yelled down. "A big rush on the curries, Rose! Two pronto!"

She listened to some strangled murmurings coming from the depths.

"They'll be a while," she told us. "She's bringing up more Gujarati sauce."

"That's given an edge to our appetites," Kenneth loftily pronounced.

In the Television Centre was the canteen block on three floors — two floors for self-serving, one on the ground floor and one on the top. In between was waitress service, serving *haute cuisine* and fine wine. And there was the BBC Club on the fourth floor, where you could get plastered and then sober up on snacks.

Down the road from the Television Centre in Wood Lane was Albertine's Wine Bar, where you could escape from office confines. It was there that Julia Smith, producer, and Tony Holland, scriptwriter, came up with *EastEnders* and — because of the inspiration of Albertine's — the main location in the soap is called Albert Square. It's gone now, upgraded to a fried chicken shop.

Stop this gourmet trail, Jeremy! That's enough of that.

Now I think of it, 'enough of that' is a useful phrase — one of those that is better said than read. Sometimes the delivery makes all the difference. For instance, if you say "I'm doing rather well," and the listener positively spits back, "Well, good for you!" — a comment laden with envy and fury — they've betrayed that they are they're not doing as well as you.

They might have got away with it in a letter.

Once, I was working with Elaine Stritch to resolve a script hiccup. I suggested we use the singular phrase 'nevertheless'.

"I *hate* that expression, Jeremy!" Stritchy barked back.

"Why?"

"There was this convention opener. The chairman declared. 'I'm pleased to announce that Mrs Gertrude Smithson Hillstein is our distinguished guest speaker...' A man in the audience shouted, 'Mrs Gertrude Smithson Hillstein is a cocksucker!' Such a slur on the guest speaker prompted a stunned silence. The chairman said, 'Nevertheless...'"

"OK, Elaine. We will say 'however'!"

Nevertheless and however, all digressions need to mercifully end, and so must this book. But you, dear reader, must have one spectral lingering question from the start of these scrawls. From the closed ladies' loo in the East Tower of the BBC TV Centre...

Who was Maureen?

A doodled Rentaghost *by Edward Brayshaw*

Afterword

by Anna Home OBE

I have known Jeremy Swan for more than fifty years. We first met at the BBC TV Children's department in the early 1960s. Jeremy was assigned as an AFM (Assistant Floor Manager) on the long-running storytelling programme *Jackanory*, where I was working as a director. He soon became a regular member of the team, directing many great storytellers, including the two with the most *Jackanory* appearances — Bernard Cribbins, and Kenneth Williams.

Jeremy went on to work on a wide range of children's programmes and we became friends as well as colleagues. At one point, I even managed to lure him away from the BBC to join me at TVS, a new regional ITV company based at Maidstone in Kent. However, after a while, he began to miss the bright lights of London and returned to TV Centre.

We were however reunited later when I also returned to the BBC to head up the Children's department.

Jeremy has always been a great storyteller. I have heard him telling his tales at many gatherings to a variety of audiences. They were always received with great enthusiasm and much enjoyed. As the years passed, these performances became increasingly polished and professional.

I said to him, "You must write these stories down. They would make a wonderful book, and more people should have the chance to enjoy them."

He didn't seem particularly keen, but I knew that he was keeping notes. He eventually gave in, and *Is That You, Maureen?* is the result.

The book is a fast-moving account of a fantastically rich life and career. Jeremy has a phenomenal memory, great powers of description, and a wonderful, sometimes wicked sense of humour. We are led through a world of stars, bars, worldwide travels, TV studios and film sets. We follow Jeremy's life from a child actor in Dublin to a successful TV professional — not also forgetting his work as an artist, cartoonist and popular guest speaker on holiday cruises.

The whole story is hugely entertaining, told with great pace and energy — leaving the reader slightly breathless, but unable to stop reading. We meet a vast range of Jeremy's friends, and colleagues, and end up feeling that they are our friends too.

This is a book to relish and return to — and I'm delighted my constant nagging paid off!

Anna Home OBE
March 2024

Homeward bound

Index

PRODUCTIONS WORKED ON BY JS

Afternoon Club (TVS) 98–100
Aladdin and the Forty Thieves (BBC) 93, 119
BBC News 48
Bluebirds (BBC) 118-119
Captain Lightfoot (film) 28
Chase Me Comrade! (BBC) 70–71
Chimes at Midnight (stage) 83
Christmas Carol, A (BBC) 95
Coast to Coast (TVS) 100
Coronation Street (Granada) 30, 40, 44–46, 76
Coronet Capers (BBC) 123
Doctor Who (BBC) 173–174
Enter Inspector Duval (film) 63
Eurovision Song Contest (RTÉ) 71–72
Farmers' Report (TVS) 100
Fraggle Rock (Henson/TVS) 98, 129, 177, 179
Galloping Galaxies (BBC) 107, 111–112
Genie from Down Under, The (ACTF/BBC) 119–121, 132
Going Live! (BBC) 119
Grandad (BBC) 89–93, 157
Handful of Songs, A (RTÉ) 71
Hedda Gabler (stage) 27–28
Jack and the Beanstalk (stage) 93–95
Jackanory (BBC) 52–59, 63–64, 66, 69, 72–73, 76–77, 106, 130, 140, 161–162, 182, 185
Jackanory Playhouse (BBC) 162

Jacks and the Beanstalk (BBC) 93
Julia Jekyll and Harriet Hyde (BBC) 123, 132–134, 177
Liffey Lane (stage) 15, 181
Magic Cuckoo Clock, The (stage) 15–17
Mikado, The (stage, in Barbados) 137–146, 180
Mix, The (BBC) 62, 65–66
Monster TV (BBC) 176–177
Play Away (BBC) 170
Play School (BBC) 53–54, 57, 170
Plough and the Stars, The (RTÉ) 105
Plum's Pots and Plans (BBC) 91–92
Potter's Picture Palace (BBC) 91
Pride and Prejudice (BBC) 48
Quartet (BBC) 59–60
Rentaghost (BBC) 9, 41–43, 89, 95, 97–98, 107, 133, 180, 182, 184
Riordans, The (RTÉ) 25, 33–34, 49–50
Round the Twist (ACTF/BBC) 112, 115–117, 120
Saint Joan (stage) 17–21, 58, 68, 73–74, 83
Secret Life of Toys, The (Henson/BBC) 129–132
Seven Year Itch, The (stage) 17, 182
Shake Hands with the Devil (film) 28
Sooty Heights (Granada) 119, 157, 177–180
Spy Who Came in from the Cold, The 33–37, 48, 63
Sudden Deaths (stage) 157–159
Tosca (stage) 136, 139, 142–144

INDEX

Treasure Houses (BBC) 102–103
Uncle Jack and... (BBC) 122–125, 129
When Santa Rode the Prairie 41
Witch Hunt (BBC) 47–48, 63
Worst Witch, The (ITV) 66

Actors' Benevolent Fund 88
Ageros, George 64, 101
AIDS 96
Alberge, Betty 42
Allen, Dave 69
Allen, Joe 103, 180–181
Andrews, Eamonn 29
Arbiter, Dickie 173
Ardmore Studios, Bray 28, 63, 66, 109
Armstrong-Jones, Anthony — see Snowdon, Tony
Ashe, Rosemary 'Rosie' 140, 144, 178
Aspel, Michael 48
Asquith, John 43, 95, 132
Aston, Bea 114
Atkins, Eileen 77
ATV, Birmingham 48
Australia 112–121, 132
Australian Children's Television Foundation (ACTF) 112, 115–116
Baker-Duly, Edward 140
Baker, Martin G. 130
Ball, Maria 59
ballet 49–50, 68–69, 77, 80, 98, 159, 161
Barbados 137–147
Barber, Albert 132
Barnes, Dorothy 78, 101–103
Barnes, Edward 64–65, 75, 77–78, 97–98, 101–103, 112
Barry, Michael 29
Baxter, Biddy 54, 116, 148–152,
Baxter, Keith 83
BBC
— Advanced Film Direction Course 63–65
— Manchester 90–93
— monitoring of Russian agents 71

— Television Centre 7, 70, 91, 95, 151–152, 182–183, 185
Bednarczyk, Stefan 140, 180
Beeching, Angela 57, 64, 75
Behrens, Julia 171
Bellinger, Chris 119
Benjamin, Floella 95, 170, 173
Bennett, Alan 59–60
Bennetts, Don 30, 43, 45–46, 115–116, 120
Bernstein, Sydney 40, 46
Bharadwaj, Monisha 171
Biggins, Christopher 9–10, 42–43, 95, 107, 114, 125–126, 136–140, 142, 144–147, 173, 180–181
Billy Elliot 128, 133–134
Binchy, Kate 105
Binder, Maurice 44
Birkbeck, Paul 57
Blake, Quentin 57
Block, Bob 42, 89, 111
Block, Madeleine 42
Bloom, Claire 36–37, 39
Blue Peter (BBC) 54, 95, 141, 149, 167, 170
Bogarde, Dirk 28–29
Bond, James 44
Brackenbury, Pat 158–159
Brayshaw, Edward 42, 95, 184
Brendan Smith Academy of Acting 15–16, 49
Brennan, Barbara 105
Brewer, Colin 34
Brown, Pam 98
Bryant, Margot 40, 45
Brychta, Jan 57
Buggy, Niall 111
Bulloch, Sally 163–164
Burnett, Barry 181
Burnett, Ewan 115
Burrowes, Norma 49–50
Burton, Richard 33–37, 39
Butt, Mohammed 'Mike' 181
Buttery, John 91
Byrne, Gay 73–74
Byrne, Paula 17

Caballé, Montserrat 49–50, 147
Cadell, Richard 178–180
Cagney, James 28
Campbell, Michael 181
Campion, Gerry 181
Cant, Brian 95
Carson, Violet 40, 45
Carty, Todd 95
Cassidy, Maura 68
Cassin, Barry 26
Casson, Glynis 56
Cassons, Kay and Christopher 13, 20–21, 28
Castle, Charles 63–65
Cavalli, Contessa Karla 140, 143
Charles, Pamela 41
Checksfield, Robert 103, 118
Chuckle, Barry and Paul 93
Ciani, Paul 41, 95
Civil, Roy 41
Clarke, Harry 44
Clarke, Maureen — see Halligan, Maureen
Clarke, Michael 44
Clarke, Sunny 44–46, 48
Cluskey, May 105
Cohen, Jonathan 55, 58
Comer, John 91
Conmee, Marie 21–22
Connor, Kenneth 95
Conroy, Maeve — later Pujorski, Maeve 29
Coogan, Pete 130
Cook, Jo 71, 161
Cooke, Nigel 111
Corbett, Poppy 159
Coronation Street (Granada) 9, 30, 40–46, 76, 119, 178
Cottrell, Helen 99
Coulter, David 55
Counsell, Elizabeth 158
Courtney, Tom 93
Coward, Shirley 47
Craven, John 95

Cribbins, Bernard 58, 161–162, 185
Crichton, David 41–42
Crime and Punishment (stage) 92–93
Crockford, Peter 139, 142
Cronin, Adrian 68
Crow, Angela 91
Cumming, Fiona 47
Curry, Mark 95–96, 102–103
Cusack, Edith 29
Dad's Army (BBC) 89, 146
Daldrey, Stephen 133–134
Dana 68
Darbyshire, Michael 42
Davies, John Howard 75
Davies, Lucy 82–83
Davis, Bette 14, 39, 173
Dawn, Liz 178
Dawson, Caroline 104, 107, 141, 152, 163–164
Dawson, John 42
de Hory, Elmyr 81–82
de' Medici, Contessa Marzia 144
Deadman, Nina 69–70
Dean, Clair 59
Dean, Lee 95
Deane, Derek 79–80, 173
Delaney, Pauline 118
Delmar, Elaine 123
Dence, Maggie 114
Dench, Dame Judi 58
Diana, Princess of Wales 80
Diffring, Anton 63
Dobbin 43–44, 95
Dodd, Ken 103
Doolan, Lelia 67, 105, 116
Doyle, Danny 71
Duggan, Wendy 75–76, 91, 100, 152
Dunbar, Norma 107
Dunn, Clive 89–92, 95, 98, 157–158
Dunn, Jackie 73–74
Dyer, Hal 42, 95
Dyke, Greg 101–102, 178
Eade, Peter 58
EastEnders (BBC) 119, 140, 183

INDEX

Edgar, Patricia 112, 115–116, 119–121
Edwards, Guy 132
Edwards, Hilton 13–15, 17–19, 27–29, 83, 105–106
Edwynn, Colin 91
Eldridge, Jim 93, 123, 177
Emery, Ann 42, 95, 114, 128, 132–134, 152, 158
Espinosa, Biddy 163
Etherington, Reg 121
European Broadcast Union (EBU) 71–72
Eurovision Song Contest (EBU) 68, 71–72
farting 7, 9–10, 43
Ferguson, Elizabeth 159
Fielding, Fenella 123–125
Fisher, Eddie 35
Fitt, Brad 139, 142, 144, 146–147
Fitz-Simon, Christopher 106
Fitzgerald, Caroline 80
Fitzgerald, Geraldine 39, 81
Floyd, Gareth 57
Fonteyn, Margot 50, 98
Forwood, Anthony 28
Foss, Hannen 64
Fox, Marilyn 64, 73, 75, 106
Fox, Mark 173
Foy, Patricia 'Paddy' 49–51, 64, 69, 76–78, 98, 116, 152
Francis, Jan 95
Fraser, Moyra 125
Fullerton, Sheelagh 106, 112
Galvin, Anna 120
George, Tricia 125
Geraghty, Clive 105
Gibbs family (Bee Gees) 81
Gibson, Chloe 29, 106, 116, 132
Gidney, Chris 167, 170–173
Goeltz, Dave 130
Gold and Silver Wyre Drawers Livery Company, the 104, 158, 167, 178
Gold, Louise 130
Goolden, Jilly 171
Gordon, Hannah 159
Grace, Janie 64

Grant, Bernie 149–150
Gray, Natasha 125
Graydon, Paul 111
Green, Robin 139
Greene, Sarah 95, 119
Greene, Simon 132
Gregory, Steven 141
Grosvenor, Angela 120, 132
Gwynne, Haydn 134
Halligan, Maureen 40, 44, 46
Hallinan, Olivia 132
Hammond, Roger 125
Hanlon, Richard 139
Hardie, Neil 104, 106, 112, 138, 158, 162–163
Hardiman, Tom 67–68
Harris, Richard 17
Hartis, Paul 130
Harty, Russell 59
Hayes, Melvyn 91, 170
Hayton, Hilary 57
Hedley, Adrian 179–180
Heller, Julek 57
Henry, Laurence 57
Henson, Brian 130
Henson, Jim 98, 129–130
Hesketh-Harvey, Kit 140
Hird, Thora 56–57, 113
Hirschfeld, Al 39–40
Hirschfeld, Nina 39–40
Hodson, Phillip 98
Hoey, Harry and Marjorie 92–93
Holland, Tony 183
Holmes, Joyce 104, 117
Holmes, Stuart 103–104, 107, 111, 117, 121, 130–131, 147, 156, 158–159, 166–173, 178, 182
Home, Anna 52, 56–57, 64–65, 73, 77, 96–97, 99–100, 102–103, 112, 115–117, 120, 130, 132, 134, 137, 162, 167, 170, 185–186
Hootkins, William 91
Hubbard, Rosin 'Ros' 80
Hudson, Rock 28
Humphries, Barry 56
Hunniford, Gloria 141

Hunter, Rita 114
Husband, Mary 146
Hutton, Barbara 85
Importance of Being Oscar, The (stage) 14
Ince, Angela 118
Irving, Edith and Clifford 82
Jackson, Anthony 42
Jackson, Peter 120
Jacques, Hattie 58
Jarman, Reginald 20
Jennings, Paul 115–117
Jensen, David 'Kid' 99
John, Elton 133–134
Johns, Glynis 28
Johnston, Jennifer 105
Johnston, Shelagh 105
Jolley, Jay 163
Jones, John 100
Jones, Paul 123, 125
Jones, Phil 120
Jordan, Diane-Louise 95, 172
Kaler, Berwick 139
Kaye, Lila 92–93
Keane, Marie 105
Keating, Caron 141
Keith, Penelope 59–60, 75–76, 123, 151
Kelly, Chris 30, 45–46
Kendall, Sue 179
Kennedy, Richard 57
Kent, Revered Cindy 173
Kenworthy, Duncan (producer) 98
Kerrigan, Michael 103, 120, 131–132
Kewley, Vanya 30, 44–46, 141–142, 152
Kidd, Johnny and Wendy 139, 145–147
La Plante, Lynda — see Marchal, Lynda
Late Late Show, The (RTÉ) 73–74
Laurie, John 89
Law, Phyllida 54–55
Lawler, Iris 22, 27–28
Lawson, Peta 115
Leach, Rosemary 56
Leahy, Carmel — aunt of JS 13–14, 67, 106
Leahy, Sheila — aunt of JS 13–14, 67, 106
Lee, Rustie 171–172

Leeming, Jan 173
Leslie, John 95, 172
Levin, Richard 'Dick' 50–51, 70, 152
Lindsay-Hogg, Eddy and Kathleen 81–82, 97, 99–100
Lindsay-Hogg, Michael 83
Lloyd Webber, Andrew 119, 173
London Weekend Television 53–55, 163
Long, Betty 20–21
Longman, Brenda 157, 178
Lowe, Shirley 118
Lowrie, Philip 40, 76
Lucas, Isabelle 118
Lumet, Sydney 39
Mac Liammóir, Micheál 12–15, 17–21, 27, 29, 37, 105–106
MacKay, Don 145-146
MacMillan, Deborah 159
Maguire, Patrick P. 106
Makower, Anne 106
Mallard, George 114
Manderson, Anna and Tim 78–79
Mandray, Jeannie 139, 141–142
Manning, Stuart 173
Marchal, Lynda — aka Lynda La Plante 42
Marks, Michael 112, 162
Marley, Patrick 125
Marlowe, Chris 171
Martelli, Angela 34
Martinez, Mina 57
Maughan, Monica 120
McAuliffe, Nichola 139–140, 142, 145–146
McCallum, Graham 57
McCutcheon, Martine 119
McGoldrick, Anna 71
McKay, Fulton 98
McKenna, Siobhán 17–18, 58, 73–74
McKern, Leo 93
McLarnon, Patrick 13, 22, 106
McLennan, Rod 56
McNeill, Josephine 21
Medford, Paul J. 140–141
Menuhin, Diana and Yehudi 76–77

INDEX

Merrifield, Blackie and Tom 161–164
Milman, Alexandra 120
Milne, Alasdair 150
Moir, James 150
Monheim Studios, Germany 130
Montague, Lee 54–55
Moran, Lona 25–26, 67, 105
Morgan, Andrew 62, 64–66, 103, 120, 131
Morgan, Jacki 62, 65
Morgan, Lucy 99
Morgan, Priscilla 98
Morley, John 93
Morris, Johnny 95
Morris, Oswald 34
Morrow, Jeff 28
Morton, Bettie 155–156
Morven, Myrette (agent of JS) 95
Muldoon, Rhys 120–121
Mullinar, Liz 120
Murray, Braham 93
Murray, Don 28
Needle, Susie 41
Negri, Pola 40, 125
Neilan, Brendan 29, 106
Nelson, Jerry 130
Nicholl, Katie 173
Nicholls, Sue 9–10, 41–43, 119
Norman, Jessye 50
Norris, Geoffrey 107
Nutkins, Terry 95
O Telefís 129
O'Connor, Caroline 125
O'Kelly, Emer 73–74
O'Reilly, Alpho 106
O'Shannon, Finnuala 105
O'Shea, Milo 17
Oldfield, Kenn 140–141
Otto, Barry 120
Owen, Christopher 124
Pattersons, The 71
Paul, Tibor 49
Pavarotti, Luciano 141, 147
Pegrum, Peter 91–92
Pemberton, Victor 98

Permutt, Stewart 125, 142, 146
Perrie, William 43, 95
Perry, Jimmy 146
Phillips, Eden 91
Phoenix, Pat 38, 40, 46
Pickard, Nigel 102
Pickles, Vivian 124–125
Pieńkowski, Jan 57
Plaskitt, Nigel 130
Plisetskaya, Maya 69
Plummer-Andrews, Theresa 'Trees' 100, 112, 116, 130
Points of View (BBC) 117
Pollard, Su 34, 56
Polo, Richard 104
Potter, Maureen 72
Pratt, Sandy 81
Prowse, John 55
Pugh, Ed 177
Pujorski, Maeve — See Conroy, Maeve
Pulman, Cory 140
Quackenbush, Alex 85–86
Quigley, Godfrey 17, 22
Quilley, Denis 139
Quinn, Mike 130
Raidió Teilifís Éireann (RTÉ) 25, 28–30, 33, 49–50, 67–69, 71–74, 82–84, 102, 105–106
Randall, Sara 158–159
Ray, Ted 56
Redgrave, Michael 28
Reid, Walter J. 139
Reynolds, Debbie 35
Rhodes, Joan 164
Richard, Cliff 141
Richards, Shelah 29, 39, 50, 67, 73–74, 81, 83, 86, 105, 116, 181
Riches, Ron 75–76, 152
Ritt, Martin 34, 36
Riverside Studios, London 47
Rix, Brian 71
Roach, William 'Bill' 40
Robertson, Liz 139–140
Robertson, Mick 170

Robinson, Eric 50
Rogers, Pieter 123
Romanov, Lev 70
Routledge, Patricia 151
Rowan, Ann 25–27
Royal Academy 164
Royal Academy of Dance 163
Royal Academy of Music 15–16
Rugheimer, Gunnar 29
Rush, Barbara 28
Rushton, Willie 41, 114
Russell, Matthew 106
Salvoni, Elena
Sandford, Brian 178
Savoy Hotel, London 58–60
Scheftel, Boy 39
Schofield, Phillip 119
Scott, Pat 13, 106
Segal, Jeffrey 42
Sell, Colin 178
Sergeant, John 173
Shallcross, Alan 59–60
Sharp, Ken 98
Sharp, Maris 139
Shea, Wendy 83, 86
Sherwood, Robert 159
Silvera, Carmen 95
Sims, Monica 41, 63–65, 72, 75, 77, 116, 127, 152
Singleton, Valerie 170
Sisson, Richard 140
Smee, Anthony 99
Smith, Diana 98, 100–101
Smith, Julia 183
Snowdon, Tony 83
Somers, Jillian 106–107, 138–139, 182
Sondheim, Stephen 139
Spears, Steve J. 120
Speed, Doris 40
Sperber, Elaine 177
Spinetti, Victor 41
Spyker, Paul 103, 133–134
St Mary's College CSSp 17, 21, 30
Staniforth, Michael 42–43, 97, 107, 180

Stapely, Sue 70–71
Star Wars 59, 91
Steafel, Sheila 118
Steiger, Rod 39
Stephens, John and Helen 178–179
Stevenson, Jocelyn 129–130
Stewart, Moira 150
Stone, Paul 64
Storm, Esben 115-116, 118–119, 120
Stritch, Elaine 58–60, 183
Stubbs, Una 99–100
Sutton, Jillie 101
Sutton, Shaun 48
Swales, Robbie 111
Swan, Giselle — sister of JS 16, 67, 106, 112
Swan, Jack — father of JS 13, 15–18, 21, 67, 80, 86, 104, 106, 130, 152, 173, 180
Swan, Jacqui — sister of JS 16, 67, 106, 112
Swan, Jeremy
— arrested 125–127
— assistant stage manager (ASM) 18, 21, 25–28, 83
— at Granada television 30, 40, 44–47, 119, 179
— at RTÉ 29–30, 33, 67-69, 71–73, 82
— at TVS 97–102, 112, 185
— attends party at Russian Embassy 69–71
— BBC Directors' course 63–66
— early stage performances 15–22
— European tour in *Saint Joan* 18–21, 68, 83
— exhibition of painting 155–156
Swan, Naomi — sister of JS 16, 67, 106, 112
Swan, Nigel — brother of JS 15–16, 21, 67, 106, 181
Swan, Una — mother of JS 13, 15–16, 18–20, 67, 86, 104, 106, 130, 152, 173
Symes, Elizabeth 115
Tallis, Nicola 173
Taylor, Elizabeth 35–37, 39, 48, 125
Television South (TVS) 97–102, 112, 185

INDEX

Theatres
— Farnham Theatre 157–158, 178
— Gaiety Theatre, Dublin 14, 17–18, 69, 72, 83
— Gate Theatre, Dublin 13, 15,17, 22, 25–27, 181-182
— Lyceum Theatre, Crewe 95
— Manor Pavilion Theatre, Sidmouth 159
— Olympia Theatre, Dublin 74, 105–106
— Théâtre de la Ville Sarah Bernhardt, Paris 18–19, 21
— Torch Theatre, Dublin 16
Thorburn, Joan 114
Thorndike, Dame Sibyl 20, 55–56
Thorogood, Maurice 157
Tobin, Brian 29
Took, Barry 95
Trowles, Tony 159
Turner, Anthea 95
Twelfth Night (stage) 139, 142
Vance, Charles and Imogen 158
Vincent, Sister Mary 40

Wagner Scott, Rosemary 139, 143
Wakeley, Richard 120
Walker, April 173
Warren, Tony 40
Watson, Rosemary 106–107, 138, 182
Webb, Steven 132
Weir, Molly 42–43, 95
Welles, Orson 82–83, 123
Westminster Abbey 103–104, 111, 147, 159, 173
Whitby, Joy 53–55
Whitehall, Michael 60
Wilce, Paul 111
Williams, Kenneth 17, 57–58, 73–74, 77, 95, 111, 118, 124, 181–182, 185
Williams, Tennessee 85
Wilson, Glenda 115
Wilson, Harold 89
Windsor, Barbara 118-119
Wogan, Terry 150
Woods, Aubrey 91
Wynter, Dana 28

THE LONG GAME

1996–2003: *THE INSIDE STORY OF HOW THE BBC BROUGHT BACK* **DOCTOR WHO**

by Paul Hayes

When Russell T Davies' triumphant *Doctor Who* relaunch hit screens in 2005, it didn't appear out of nowhere – the show's journey back to television was long and complicated. The years since the last revival attempts saw enormous changes at the BBC, not least in the Drama department; along with battles between different parts of the Corporation over who should bring the Doctor back; and even doubts over whether the BBC still held the rights to make the show.

The Long Game is the story of those conflicts and setbacks, during a transformative time for the BBC. It's a story told by those who were there, including BBC One Controllers Lorraine Heggessey and Alan Yentob, drama bosses Julie Gardner, Jane Tranter and Mal Young, BBC Worldwide executives Rupert Gavin and Mike Phillips, and BBC Films head David Thompson – many speaking in depth for the first time about their part in the attempts to bring back *Doctor Who*.

Drawing on dozens of interviews and extensive research, *The Long Game* tells how *Doctor Who* went from a one-night stand in May 1996 to a headline-making major recommission in September 2003.

ISBN: 978-1-908630-80-3

Biddy Baxter

THE WOMAN WHO MADE **BLUE PETER**

by Richard Marson

Biddy Baxter is a television legend — more famous than many of the stars of *Blue Peter*, the BBC mainstay she ran for over a quarter of a century. Her extraordinary drive and obsessional dedication transformed the show into the world's longest-running and most successful children's programme — with its rich mix of action, adventure, appeals, animals, exploration, studio spectaculars and things to cook and make.

At a time when very few women reached the top, Biddy — powerful, stylish and uncompromising — used her power and skill to shape the hearts and minds of generations of British children. Loved by some, loathed by others — what was she really like, and how did she achieve such success?

Richard Marson tells Biddy's story against the evolving backdrop of *Blue Peter*, drawing on over 100 exclusive interviews, Biddy's private archive, and his own inside knowledge of the programme. The book also contains dozens of previously unpublished photographs.

ISBN: 978-1-908630-31-5

TOTALLY TASTELESS
THE LIFE OF JOHN NATHAN-TURNER

by Richard Marson

'The definitive behind-the-scenes portrait of *Doctor Who* in the 80s; densely researched, eminently readable. Marson has talked to almost every key player.' *The Times*

For more than a decade, producer John Nathan-Turner, or 'JN-T' as he was often known, was in charge of every major artistic and practical decision affecting *Doctor Who*, the world's longest-running science fiction programme.

Richard Marson brings his dramatic, farcical, sometimes scandalous, often moving story to life with the benefit of his own inside knowledge and the fruits of over 100 revealing interviews with key friends and colleagues, from those John loved to those from whom he became estranged. The author has also had access to all of Nathan-Turner's surviving archive of paperwork and photos, many of which appear here for the very first time.

Includes a new afterword, gathering thoughts and tributes from John's friends and colleagues, along with previously unseen photographs.

ISBN: 978-1-908630-40-7

The author

JEREMY SWAN began his career as a child actor in the Dublin Gate Theatre, working for Hilton Edwards and Micheál Mac Liammóir. At a tender age, he had played in every major capital's theatre as the Page in *Saint Joan*, starring Siobhán McKenna.

After working as a theatre stage manager and scenic artist he joined the Irish film industry at Ardmore Studios as an assistant director, where he worked on *The Spy Who Came in from the Cold*, starring Richard Burton.

From Irish Television's RTÉ he moved to Granada TV in 1966, working on *Coronation Street* as a floor manager. He subsequently joined BBC Children's Programmes, initially directing *Jackanory* with such stalwarts as Kenneth Williams, Bernard Cribbins, Judi Dench, George Layton, Thora Hird, Christopher Biggins, Geraldine McEwan, Phylida Law, Su Pollard, Maurice Denham, Penelope Keith, John Laurie, Elaine Stritch and Richard Wattis.

Jeremy became the producer of the popular series *Rentaghost*, *Grandad* starring Clive Dunn and *Potter's Picture Palace* starring Melvyn Hayes. He directed *Play Away*, the *Blue Peter* pantomimes, and wrote and produced *Julia Jekyll and Harriet Hyde*. He produced *Bad Boyes* and *Uncle Jack*, both written by Jim Eldridge. For Jim Henson Productions, he directed *The Secret Life of Toys* and for ITV, he directed *Art Attack*, *Sooty* and *Fraggle Rock*.

In Australia, he worked on *Round the Twist* as a producer and directed *The Genie from Down Under*.

Jeremy's work as an exhibition artist inspired him to write his first stage play, *Sudden Deaths*, produced at the 24th Summer Play Season in Sidmouth. He's still writing and painting — everything from walls to Christmas cards.